Self
Work 101

Copyright © 2023 Bianca Gibson

All rights reserved. No part of this publication may be reproduced, distributed, or transmitted in any form or by any means, including photocopying, recording, or other electronic or mechanical methods, without the prior written permission of the publisher, except in the case of brief quotations embodied in critical reviews and certain other noncommercial uses permitted by copyright law. For permission requests, write to the publisher, addressed "Attention: Permissions Coordinator," at the address below.

All definitions in this book have been sourced from www.dictionary.com, www.google.com, www.merriam-webster.com and www.oed.com.

ISBN: 978-1-63616-134-1

Published By Opportune Independent Publishing Co.
www.opportunepublishing.com

Printed in the United States of America

For permission requests, please email the publisher with the subject line as "Attention: Permissions Coordinator"
to the email address below:

Info@Opportunepublishing.com

DEDICATION

This book is dedicated to my son, Ma'Kiyah Cheney, first and foremost. On January 22, 2002, at approximately 2:12 PM, he made his grand entrance into this unpredictable world. At age 20, I had not experienced true love until I held my son in my arms for the very first time. At that very moment, my life changed forever, and I began to demonstrate an unwavering commitment to him like never before. I know that I birthed you, son, but you gave me life and purpose. Ma'Kiyah, I love you infinity!

Secondly, I dedicate this SELF workbook to myself and my travels. Unknowingly, until now, maybe my readers were not aware that the majority of this workbook was written during my travels around the world. With over 20 years of traveling experience, I indulge in self-care, self-reflection, self-motivation, solitude, and more. I'd also add that even during some struggles and troublesome times in my life, I was inspired to encourage others through my powerful life experiences as I've shared briefly throughout this workbook. My travels have inspired me in so many ways, and they were the most enjoyable and peaceful times of my life, which makes this SELF book so inspiring and meaningful to share with you. It is my hope that you gain more understanding of your life through the innovative education that this book has to offer. I also wish you well on your 101-day journey of self-awareness, self-reflection, self-motivation, and ultimately self-care as you discover, rediscover, and/or implement the new and refreshed embarkment of SELF.

–Gentle Regards
Bianca G.

Over the next 101 days, we will identify, explore, and enhance our lives by indulging in self-care, self-love, self-esteem, and self-confidence. No matter which day you receive this booklet, your 365-day journey starts when you decide it's time. It is vital that you take this journey seriously and be consistent with your daily attendance to receive the full potential of your growth. I, too, will utilize this workbook for 101 days.

Our 101 SELF begins now!

TABLE OF CONTENTS

8	Self-esteem
10	Exploring Self-esteem
12	Self-love
14	Experience
16	Determination
18	Unique(ness)
20	Self-confidence
21	Strength
23	Growth
25	Self-care
27	Consistency
29	Experiences
31	Persistence
33	Manifestation
35	Motivation
37	Self-discipline
39	Growth Part 2:
41	Self-awareness
43	Choosing
45	Balance
47	Resilience
49	Change
51	Serenity
53	Mindfulness
55	Reward
57	Self-discipline Part 2:
59	Elevation
61	Calmness
63	Relaxation
65	Manifestation Part 2:
67	Self-assurance
69	Peace
71	Healing
73	Comfort
75	Dignity
77	Self-admiration
79	Beauty
81	Courage
83	Inspiration
85	Determination Part 2:
87	Perseverance
89	Understanding
91	Self-concept
93	Wisdom
95	Knowledge
97	Responsibility
99	Mindset
101	Accountability
103	Realization
105	Empath

107 Wellness	162 Impact
109 Purpose	164 Nurture
111 Self-educate	166 Preparation
113 Boldness	168 Transformation
115 Evaluation	170 Reset
117 Self-discovery	172 Transition
119 Attitude	174 Transparency
121 Self-investment	176 Execution
123 Potential	178 Vision
125 Renew	180 Productivity
127 Fierce	182 Pursuit
129 Insight	184 Stability
131 Energy	186 Intrigued
133 Ambition	188 Envision
135 Meditation	190 Diligence
137 Critical Thinking	192 Embody
139 Influence	194 Patience
142 Reevaluate	196 Assertiveness
144 Explore	198 Tranquility
146 Mentality	200 Possibility
148 Venture	202 Bravery
150 Power	204 Receptive
152 Self-respect	206 Modest
154 Feel(ings)	208 Freedom
156 Commitment	
158 Ability	
160 Evolution	

What better time to start your love discipline than now? What is it that you desire to gain from this journey?

_____

_____

_____

_____

The 365 on Me questionnaire is designed for you to be open and honest with yourself, for yourself. If you check "Undecided" on any of the questionnaires, please refer to the back of the book and provide further explanation so that you can explore confusion, define uncertainty, and confront any doubt that could be restricting and causing you to be withheld from your own potential.

One day, you will wake up and realize you were not who you want to be; or another day, you will go to sleep pondering about how to create a 'new' you.

– Bianca G.

Self-esteem |self-es·teem| - a confidence and satisfaction in oneself.

LESSON QUESTION
In your own words, what is the meaning of self-esteem?

_____

_____

365 ON ME QUESTIONNAIRE
1. Do you believe that you have what it requires to become who you desire to be?
   Yes
   No
   Undecided

2. If you were asked to demonstrate self-love, would you be able to do so?
   Yes
   No
   Undecided

REMINDER
Regardless of your experience today, put one foot before the other, and keep moving.
—Bianca G.

INSPIRATIONAL QUOTE
"The sun does not ask permission to shine, and neither do I."
– Erica Gerald Mason

SUMMARY
Please write your demonstration of self-love today.

Welcome to day 2, loves!

Now that we have gotten fired up, let's start exploring self-esteem. Let's take a moment to reflect. Close your eyes for a minute or two and visualize yourself as your best you. What does this look like for you?

_____

_____

_____

LESSON QUESTION
When visualizing your best you, what was your first thought (e.g. an actual picture, inspirational words, accomplishments)?

_____

_____

_____

365 ON ME QUESTIONNAIRE
1. What does it mean to explore your self-esteem?
    - An opened door to new opportunities
    - Defining your true self-love
    - Demonstrating who you desire to be

2. Did you know that self-esteem is what you believe it is?
    - Yes
    - No
    - Undecided

REMINDER
Be consistent in all that you engage to improve self-care. Stay true to who you are. Even if you haven't figured it out yet, believe that one day, you will, so stick to the discovery plan.

—Bianca G.

INSPIRATIONAL QUOTE
"Discipline will multiply everything in your life."
— Via Park Secrets

SUMMARY
Please write your demonstration of self-love today.

_____

_____

_____

_____

_____

_____

_____

_____

_____

_____

_____

_____

_____

_____

Every day, you will experience different emotions, and sometimes, many different emotions all in the same day. Take a deep breath, even take a break, and then hit the reset button because this moment will only last as long as you allow it to.

– Bianca G.

S – Secure a safe place
E – Esoterical approach
L – Love
F – Forever and embrace the ability to
L – Learn
O – Omnipotent and
V – Viable
E – Everlasting strength in loving YOU!

Self-love |self-'ləv| - Love of self, such as an appreciation of one's own worth or virtue.

LESSON QUESTION
In your own words, what is the meaning of self-love?

_____

_____

_____

365 ON ME QUESTIONNAIRE
1. In all that you encounter in this life, is there one single belief in everlasting self-love?
   Yes
   No
   Undecided

REMINDER
This life did not come with a manual. Therefore, pick a day, a time, and even a place to live for yourself, and continue to do it so that you will never miss a beep.

–Bianca G.

INSPIRATIONAL QUOTE
"You alone are enough. You have nothing to prove to anybody."
— Maya Angelou

SUMMARY
Please write your demonstration of self-love today.

_____
_____
_____
_____
_____
_____
_____
_____
_____
_____
_____
_____
_____
_____
_____

"If you don't write about it, was it really worth it?"

— Jensen McRae

PERSONAL REFLECTION
March 20th, 2022.
Meanwhile, on vacation with my niece, walking the streets of LA, I spotted this quote on the ground. I immediately pulled out my phone and snapped a quick pic. I've always enjoyed writing and taking pictures, so a lot like this quote, I believe that moments are worth capturing, either by writing about them or simply taking photos to commemorate the experiences. I chose to do both.

LESSON QUESTION
Have you kept a journal? If so, how often do you write about your emotions? If not, would you consider starting to work on your self-care goals?

_____

_____

_____

365 ON ME QUESTIONNAIRE
1. Does writing about your self-love experiences help you improve and/or encourage new ideas?
    Yes
    No
    Undecided

2. When setting self-care goals, would you consider writing inspirational words?
    Yes
    No
    Undecided

REMINDER
Memories help us to reflect on the past while pressing forward the future. Although the time has passed, reflect often to remember it. Hopefully, you're going to reflect on happy and joyful times so that you can experience even more.

INSPIRATIONAL QUOTE

"Do it again and again. Consistency makes the raindrops to create holes in the rock. Whatever is difficult can be done easily with regular attendance, attention, and action."

– Israelmore Ayivor

SUMMARY

Please write your demonstration of self-love today.

Determination is getting up every day and doing what has to be done. Dedication is repeatedly doing what needs to be done. Consistency is continuously doing what must be done, even when you don't feel motivated to get it done.

– Bianca G.

LESSON QUESTION
What drives you to get things done when you don't feel like it?

_____

_____

_____

365 ON ME QUESTIONNAIRE
1. Do you believe that self-love and self-care promote motivation in your life?
   Yes
   No
   Undecided

2. When you are not feeling your best, do you engage in self-care activities to feel better?
   Yes
   No
   Undecided

3. Does reading positive affirmations encourage you to practice self-love?
   Yes
   No
   Undecided

REMINDER
There will be days when you don't feel like getting things done. On these days, take necessary breaks to allow yourself time to replenish. When you are feeling better, hit the reset button and get back into it.

–Bianca G.

INSPIRATIONAL QUOTE

"Do it again and again. Consistency makes the raindrops to create holes in the rock. Whatever is difficult can be done easily with regular attendance, attention, and action."
– Israelmore Ayivor

SUMMARY

Please write your demonstration of self-love today.

_____
_____
_____
_____
_____
_____
_____
_____
_____
_____
_____
_____
_____
_____

The beauty of being you alone is what makes you unique. With billions of people in the world, you're the only person that gets to be you. Think about how awesome it is to be who you are and all that comes with being you.

– Bianca G.

LESSON QUESTION
What makes you unique?

_____

_____

_____

     Y - You are your greatest project to be,
     O - Obedient to what you set forth to accomplish and be,
     U - Unique.

365 ON ME QUESTIONNAIRE
1. Does being you require approval of others?
    Yes
    No
    Undecided

2. Are there some things about you that you'd like to change to become your "best" self?
    Yes
    No
    Undecided

REMINDER
There are so many people who are constantly being told what they should do to be "better." Self-confidence proves that you're the only one who gets to decide what require you to be the best you that you can be.

– Bianca G.

INSPIRATIONAL QUOTE

"To be yourself in a world that is constantly trying to make you something else is the greatest accomplishment."

– Ralph Waldo Emerson

SUMMARY

Please write your demonstration of self-love today.

_____
_____
_____
_____
_____
_____
_____
_____
_____
_____
_____
_____
_____
_____
_____
_____
_____

Self-confidence | self-'kän-fə-dən(t)s | - confidence in oneself and in one's powers and abilities.

POSITIVE AFFIRMATIONS BY YOURS TRULY:

Never shrink yourself to fit in small spaces.

Even when you're not sure of all that you're capable of, choose to believe in who you are and possibilities.

Crown yourself queen or king, and if or when you feel unsure, readjust your crown and keep going.

LESSON QUESTION

Even on the most challenging days, what contributes to your self-confidence?

_____

_____

_____

_____

INSPIRATIONAL QUOTE

"If you're always trying to be normal, you will never know how amazing you can be."
– Maya Angelou

SUMMARY

Please write your demonstration of self-love today.

_____

_____

_____

_____

_____

Strength often requires one to stretch their wings and fly, even during the toughest times. In this life, we must learn that there is power in believing that you can persevere in spite of opposition.

– Bianca G.

LESSON QUESTION
Are there times when you have demonstrated strength that you didn't know you possessed? If so, please share.

_____

_____

_____

365 ON ME QUESTIONNAIRE
1. Do you believe that you possess strength that you're not aware of?
    Yes
    No
    Undecided

2. Are there times when you feel stronger than you've ever felt before?
    Yes
    No
    Undecided

REMINDER
Whatever you believe about yourself is only as true as you allow it to be, so be your kind of truth.

– Bianca G.

INSPIRATIONAL QUOTE
"When I dare to be powerful, to use my strength in the service of my vision, then it becomes less and less important whether I am afraid."

– Audre Lorde

SUMMARY
Please write your demonstration of self-love today.

"To plant a seed, watch it grow, to tend it and then harvest it, offered a simple but enduring satisfaction. The sense of being the custodian of the small patch of earth offered a taste of freedom."

— Nelson Mandela

POSITIVE AFFIRMATIONS:

"It was crowded on the elevator. I took the stairs."

— Lil Baby, Dominique Jones

"There are no shortcuts to the top of the palm tree."

— African Proverb

LESSON QUESTION

What is your definition of personal growth? What will it take for you to get to where you desire to be in this life?

_____

_____

_____

_____

365 ON ME QUESTIONNAIRE

1. Are there things and people that I am allowing to hold me back from becoming the greatest version of myself?
    Yes
    No
    Undecided

2. Do my circumstances require elimination of people and things that are impeding my growth?
    Yes
    No
    Undecided

REMINDER
Sometimes, endings are new beginnings.

— Bianca G.

INSPIRATIONAL QUOTE
"To reach your potential, you must grow. And to grow, you must be highly intentional about it."

— John C. Maxwell

SUMMARY
Please write your demonstration of self-love today.

_____

_____

_____

_____

_____

_____

_____

_____

_____

_____

_____

_____

"Self-care doesn't always have to reflect tangible value but more so, what you feel on the inside that contributes to every aspect of your life."

– Bianca G.

Self-care | self-'ker | - care for oneself.

POSITIVE AFFIRMATIONS:
I am successful.
I am confident.
I am powerful.
I am strong.
I am an unstoppable force of nature.

– Bianca G.

LESSON QUESTION
What is your personal definition of self-care?

_____

_____

Identify five different self-care activities you currently practice or want to start.

_____   _____   _____

_____   _____

365 ON ME QUESTIONNAIRE
1. Am I allowing my financial status to determine how and when I engage in self-care?
    Yes
    No
    Undecided

2. Does practicing self-care have anything to do with tangible things?
    Yes
    No
    Undecided

A FEW SELF-CARE IDEAS
Drink herbal tea
Sleep
Watch the sunrise
Walk in nature
Make a vision board
Drink water
Stretch
Do yoga poses
Go for a walk
Journal

— Bianca G.

INSPIRATIONAL QUOTE
"Being in love with every part of yourself. Taking care of your needs and not sacrificing your well-being to please others. Not settling for less than you deserve."
— Maya Angelou

SUMMARY
Please write your demonstration of self-love.

_____

_____

_____

_____

_____

_____

_____

_____

When given the opportunity, rewrite your story. You can add to it as many times as you'd like; just remember that consistency helps to produce positive results.

– Bianca G.

Consistency | kən-ˈsi-stən(t)-sē | - an agreement or harmony of parts of features to one another or a whole.

LESSON QUESTION
What can you do to ensure consistency in your self-care activities?

_____

_____

Identify five different, consistent behaviors that you can practice to engage in self-care. (ex. create a regimen/routine)

_____   _____   _____

_____   _____

365 ON ME QUESTIONNAIRE
1. Am I allowing other things, people, and/or my hesitation to hold me back from practicing self-care?
   Yes
   No
   Undecided

2. Do I need others' experiences and encouragement to practice more self-care?
   Yes
   No
   Undecided

REMINDER
A tree must receive water and sun to flourish. There are 4 stages in the tree growth process (seed, stem, sapling, and full-grown tree). Like a tree, we flourish when we are consistent and receiving care, love, and support from self. Continue to water your soil (soul) and dance in the sun(light), even when you don't feel like it. Consistency produces growth.

– Bianca G.

INSPIRATIONAL QUOTE
"Success is the sum of small efforts, repeated day in and day out."
— Robert Collier

SUMMARY
Please write your demonstration of self-love.

_____

_____

_____

_____

_____

_____

_____

_____

_____

_____

_____

_____

_____

_____

_____

_____

"A winner is a dreamer who never gives up."

– Nelson Mandela

POSITIVE REFLECTION

Often in life, we go through ups, downs, and trials that this life has offered us. For some reason, we're able to recall our circumstances, but we tend not to commemorate more "happy" times. Let's stop this unhealthy habit and create a positive regime. TODAY, you will start to reflect on the happiness and/or success you have experienced. See below for details.

– Bianca G.

List a year in which you experienced happiness and success. Here are a few examples to help you focus on what's important to you.
Ex. Year 2012 – graduated with honors
Ex. Year 2017 – got married
Ex. Year 2021 – overcame depressive thoughts

Year _____ — _____

Year _____ — _____

Year _____ — _____

365 ON ME QUESTIONNAIRE

1. Am I holding myself back from experiencing the life that I deserve to have?
    Yes
    No
    Undecided

REMINDER

Remember, if you are not using it, you could be losing it. If you dream it, you can become it. If you want it, go get it!

– Bianca G.

INSPIRATIONAL QUOTE

"Winning is fun, sure. But winning is not the point. Wanting to win is the point. Not giving up is the point. Never letting up is the point. Never being satisfied with what you've done is the point."

– Pat Summit

SUMMARY

Please write your demonstration of self-love today.

_____
_____
_____
_____
_____
_____
_____
_____
_____
_____
_____
_____
_____
_____

"Thankfully, persistence is a great substitute for talent."

– Steve Martin

Persistence | pər-ˈsi-stən(t)s | - the quality or state of being persistent–tenacious.

LESSON QUESTION
What is your definition of persistence?

_____

_____

365 ON ME QUESTIONNAIRE
1. Is there anything impeding my ability to become who I desire to be?
    Yes
    No
    Undecided

2. Have I allowed past failures or mishaps to halt my ability to feel confident in my abilities?
    Yes
    No
    Undecided

REMINDER
You're only as good as you desire to be.

– Bianca G.

INSPIRATIONAL QUOTE
"Some people want it to happen, some wish it would happen, others make it happen."

– Michael Jordan

SUMMARY
Please write your demonstration of self-love today.

"I am attracting better because I have discovered that it all starts with me. I am going to change myself first so that everything aligns for me. I am not going to blame anyone. I am going to take responsibility for my life. The better I become, the better I attract."

– Unknown

Manifestation | ma-nə-fə-ˈstā-shən | - the act, process, or an instance of manifesting– bringing your desires to fruition.

LESSON QUESTION

What have you manifested in your life?
_____
_____
_____

What do you desire to manifest in your life?
_____
_____
_____

How to Manifest by Shakira Maria:
1. Decide what you want.
2. Feel the energy of your desire.
3. Visualize your desire.
4. Release limiting beliefs.
5. Believe in your ability to manifest.
6. Take inspired action.
7. Allow the process to unfold.

365 ON ME QUESTIONNAIRE

1. Am I capable of manifesting my desire?
    Yes
    No
    Undecided

REMINDER
Clarity + Alignment + Action = Manifestation

Complete manifestation sentences:

I will _____.

I can _____.

I am _____.

I have _____.

I know _____.

INSPIRATIONAL QUOTE
"Instead of trying to build a brick wall, lay a brick everyday. Eventually, you'll look up, and you'll have a brick wall."

– Nipsey Hustle

SUMMARY
Please write your demonstration of self-love today.

_____

_____

_____

_____

_____

_____

_____

_____

"Do what you have to do until you can do what you want to do."

– Oprah Winfrey

Motivation | mō-tə-ˈvā-shən | - the general desire or willingness of someone to do something.

In your own words, what is the meaning of motivation?

_____

_____

LESSON QUESTION
What motivates you and why?

_____

_____

_____

365 ON ME QUESTIONNAIRE
1. Do I lack self-motivation?
   - Yes
   - No
   - Undecided

2. Are there positive influences that I seek out to motivate me?
   - Yes
   - No
   - Undecided

REMINDER
What I desire is on the opposite side of my obstacles.

– Bianca G.

INSPIRATIONAL QUOTE
"When you have a $1 million vision, don't surround yourself with 1-cent minds.
— Unknown

SUMMARY
Please write your demonstration of self-love today.

_____
_____
_____
_____
_____
_____
_____
_____
_____
_____
_____
_____
_____
_____
_____
_____

One's ability to know their struggles, plan their success, execute their goals, and visualize their outcome demonstrates self-qualifications of self-discipline.

— Bianca G.

Self-discipline | self-ˈdi-sə-plən | - the ability to control one's feelings to overcome one's weaknesses.

In your own words, what is the meaning of self-discipline?

_____

_____

LESSON QUESTION
What behaviors have I displayed that demonstrate self-discipline?

_____

_____

365 ON ME QUESTIONNAIRE
1. Do I deserve to possess more characteristics of self-discipline?
   Yes
   No
   Undecided

2. Are there any people, places, or things that distract me from practicing self-discipline?
   Yes
   No
   Undecided

REMINDER
"Self-control is the war between impulsivity and doing what's right or beneficial. It's the ability to control emotions, impulses, or behaviors to achieve a greater goal."

— Unknown

INSPIRATIONAL QUOTE
"With self-discipline, most anything is possible."
— Theodore Roosevelt

SUMMARY
Please write your demonstration of self-love today.

_____

_____

_____

_____

_____

_____

_____

_____

_____

_____

_____

_____

_____

_____

"Without change, nothing would grow, and without growth, nothing would survive."
— Unknown

Growth | ˈgrōth | - the process of increasing in physical size.

POSITIVE QUOTE
"Know, first, who you are, and then adorn yourself accordingly."
— Epictetus

LESSON QUESTION
In what area(s) of your life have you recognized growth?

_____

_____

365 ON ME QUESTIONNAIRE
1. Am I growing in significant areas in my life?
    Yes
    No
    Undecided

2. Are there specific areas in my life that I'd like to grow more?
    Yes
    No
    Undecided

REMINDER
"Growth doesn't come from comfort zones."
— Bianca G.

INSPIRATIONAL QUOTE
"To reach your potential you must grow. And to grow, you must be highly intentional about it."
— John C. Maxwell

SUMMARY
Please write your demonstration of self-love today.

"Self-awareness doesn't stop you from making mistakes. It allows you to learn from them."
— Unknown

Self-awareness | self-ə-'wer-nəs | - conscious knowledge of one's own character, feelings, motives, and desires.

THE 5 ELEMENTS OF SELF-AWARENESS BY JESS SEXTON
- Self-concept: Your perception of you. Your perceptions come from your personal experiences, what you expect from yourself in the future, and what you believe your abilities are.
- Thoughts: Our thoughts are tied to our emotions, so when we try to become more aware of our emotions, we must first understand our thoughts and thought process.
- Feelings: How do you feel when you say things about yourself? What about when other people say things about you? No matter what your feelings are, you must identify which are associated with your thoughts and experiences.
- Body: Sometimes, when we're thinking, it comes with a physical response that other people may or may not notice!
- Emotions are the most powerful factor in how we interact with others. People with higher levels of emotional intelligence are able to recognize and accept their varying emotional states.

365 ON ME QUESTIONNAIRE
1. Am I self-aware?
   Yes
   No
   Undecided

REMINDER
"I am whoever I believe I am."
— Bianca G.

INSPIRATIONAL QUOTE
"Self-awareness gives you the capacity to learn from your mistakes, as well as your success. It enables you to keep growing."
— Lawrence Bossidy

SUMMARY
Please write your demonstration of self-love today.

"Every choice comes with a consequence. Once you make a choice, you must accept responsibility. You cannot escape the consequences of your choices, whether you like them or not."

– Roy T. Bennett

Choosing | ˈchüz | - an act of selecting or making a decision when faced with two or more possibilities.

C – Choose
H – How
O – Opportunity
I – Influences your
C – Choice or your
E – Ego

"The 3 Cs of Life: Choices, chances, changes. You must make a choice to take a chance, or your life will never change."

– Unknown

LESSON QUESTION

When you make a choice, what is it influenced by? Your perception or others' perceptions?

_____

_____

365 ON ME QUESTIONNAIRE

1. Do I have difficulties with making appropriate decisions?
    Yes
    No
    Undecided

REMINDER

"Making a decision seems difficult at times. Well, being able to live with your decisions could be even more challenging, so choose wisely."

– Bianca G.

INSPIRATIONAL QUOTE
"Life is a matter of choices, and every choice you make makes you."
– John C. Maxwell

SUMMARY
Please write your demonstration of self-love today.

"Life is all about balance. You don't always need to be getting stuff done. Sometimes, it's perfectly okay, and absolutely necessary, to shut down, kick back, and do nothing."

– Unknown

Finding balance in life helps to improve many areas of your life, physically, financially, emotionally, mentally, and spiritually. Balance is vital to improve your overall health.

– Bianca G.

Balance | ˈba-lən(t)s | -an even distribution of weight, enabling someone or something to remain upright and steady.

LESSON QUESTION
How can I create a steady balance in my life?

Physically _____

Emotionally _____

Mentally _____

Financially _____

Spiritually _____

365 ON ME QUESTIONNAIRE
1. Are there one or two areas in which I need to create balance in my life, more so than others?
    - Yes
    - No
    - Undecided

REMINDER
Balance creates opportunities, opportunity welcomes experience, and experience offers freedom.

– Bianca G.

INSPIRATIONAL QUOTE
"Live a life that is well balanced; don't do things in excess."

– Daniel Smith

SUMMARY

Please write your demonstration of self-love today.

"Courage is not the absence of fear, but rather the judgment that something else is more important than fear."
— Ambrose Redmoon

Resilience | ri-ˈzil-yən(t)s | - the capacity to recover quickly from difficulties; toughness.

LESSON QUESTION
Name something that you have overcome, and as a result, you demonstrated resilience.

_____

_____

365 ON ME QUESTIONNAIRE
1. Have I mistaken my ability to be resilient with something else?
   Yes
   No
   Undecided

2. Is there anything that can be hindering me and/or keeping me from being my strongest self?
   Yes
   No
   Undecided

REMINDER
Even in the midst of adversity, where we experience darkness, there is hope to light the path we take while this journey continues.
— Bianca G.

INSPIRATIONAL QUOTE
"The ultimate measure of a man is not where he stands in the moments of comfort and convenience, but where he stands at times of challenge in controversy."
— Martin Luther King Jr.

SUMMARY
Please write your demonstration of self-love today.

"There is nothing permanent except change."
— Heraclitus

Change | ˈchānj | - the ability to make someone or something different; alter or modify.

"Change is inevitable. Growth is optional."
— John C. Maxwell

LESSON QUESTION
What areas (mentally, romantically, physically, financially, emotionally, spiritually, etc.), of my life demand a change?

_____

_____

_____

_____

365 ON ME QUESTIONNAIRE
1. Am I allowing fear to hold me back from making the change(s) I know I need to make?
    Yes
    No
    Undecided

REMINDER
Change can be unpredictable, sudden and even scary at times. It takes courage to move from a comfortable situation. Just remember, growth develops when we choose to water our flowers while in the waiting season. More plants will flourish.
— Bianca G.

INSPIRATIONAL QUOTE
"Man cannot discover new oceans, unless he has the courage to lose sight of the shore."
— Andre Cide

SUMMARY

Please write your demonstration of self-love today.

Experiencing peace, quiet and calmness in this busy world can be very challenging, therefore we have to make up our minds and choose serenity over all things.

— Bianca G.

Serenity | sə-ˈre-nə-tē | - the state of being calm, peaceful, and untroubled.

POSITIVE QUOTE
"Serenity is not freedom from the storm, but peace amid the storm."
— S. A. Jefferson-Wright

LESSON QUESTION
Describe what it means to experience serenity in your life.

_____

_____

_____

365 ON ME QUESTIONNAIRE
1. Are there people and/or things that I am allowing to impede my experience of serenity?
    Yes
    No
    Undecided

REMINDER
You can choose what your peace will look like for you. Once you've decided, take time to enjoy the stillness and tranquility in this world.
— Bianca G.

INSPIRATIONAL QUOTE
"Radiate an energy of serenity and peace, so that you have an uplifting effort on those you come in contact with."
—Dr. Wayne Dyer

SUMMARY
Please write your demonstration of self-love today.

I inhale positive energy and exhale any fears.
I will not worry about things that are out of my control.
I am no longer afraid of what could go wrong.
I focus on what is going right.
I will calmly think of solutions to any problems that may arise.
I can handle anything that comes my way.

– Unknown

Mindfulness | ˈmīn(d)-fəl-nəs | - the quality or state of being conscious or aware of something.

LESSON QUESTION

Have you experienced mindfulness? If so, share your experience. If not, or if you're not sure, describe what you'd like your mindfulness experience to be.

_____

_____

_____

365 ON ME QUESTIONNAIRE

1. Are you truly present in your life (aware and paying attention to what's happening)?
   Yes
   No
   Undecided

REMINDER

Whatever you focus your attention on becomes who you are. So, be wise and acknowledge all things so that you are aware of and present in your life.

– Bianca G.

INSPIRATIONAL QUOTE

"Mindfulness is a way of being present: paying attention to and accepting what is happening in our lives. It helps us to be aware of and step away from our automatic and habitual reactions to our everyday experiences."
— Elizabeth Thornton

"If it's out of your hands, it deserves freedom from your mind too."
— Ivan Nuru

SUMMARY

Please write your demonstration of self-love today.

_____

_____

_____

_____

_____

_____

_____

_____

_____

_____

_____

_____

"The highest reward for a person's toil is not what they get for it, but what they become by it."
— John Ruskin

Reward | ˈmīn(d)-fəl-nəs | - anything given in recognition of one's service, effort, or achievement.

Whatsoever one deserves, the pleasure from their own good works, that person shall receive without hesitation.
— Bianca G.

LESSON QUESTION
How often do you celebrate yourself after you have completed a milestone and/or task, or just because?

_____

_____

365 ON ME QUESTIONNAIRE
1. Do I reward myself as much as I should?
    Yes
    No
    Undecided

REMINDER
Sometimes, rewarding yourself can be as simple as taking a long walk in nature, meditating, getting a massage, traveling, quoting positive affirmations, and so much more. You decide how you give yourself flowers.
— Bianca G.

INSPIRATIONAL QUOTE
"For every disciplined effort, there is a multiple reward."
— Jim Rohn

SUMMARY
Please write your demonstration of self-love today.

"Self-discipline is the ability to make yourself do what you should do, when you should do it, whether you feel like it or not."

– Elbert Hubbard

Self-discipline | ˌself-ˈdi-sə-plən | - the ability to control one's feelings and overcome one's weaknesses; the ability to pursue what one thinks is right despite temptations to abandon it.

LESSON QUESTION

How do I practice self-discipline in my life?

_____

_____

_____

What areas of my life do I need to practice self-discipline?

_____

_____

_____

365 ON ME QUESTIONNAIRE

1. Are there areas in my life where self-discipline is not evident?
   Yes
   No
   Undecided

REMINDER

Discipline yourself to do the things that need to be done. Take necessary breaks, but don't quit.

–Bianca G.

INSPIRATIONAL QUOTE
"Self-discipline is when your conscience tells you to do something and you don't talk back."

– W. K. Hope

SUMMARY
Please write your demonstration of self-love today.

_____
_____
_____
_____
_____
_____
_____
_____
_____
_____
_____
_____
_____
_____
_____

In this life, we must learn to separate to elevate. Elevation requires a new height and a brand new perspective. Make sure you're equipped for the highest climb.

– Bianca G.

Elevation | ˌe-lə-ˈvā-shən | - the height to which something is.

LESSON QUESTION
Have you recently evaluated your life and noticed the need for separation from a person, place, and/or thing? Please explain.

_____

_____

_____

365 ON ME QUESTIONNAIRE
1. Does your next level of growth require separation from a person?
   Yes
   No
   Undecided

2. Does your next level of elevation require separation from a specific situation?
   Yes
   No
   Undecided

REMINDER
There will be moments in your life where you will experience isolation. In these times, evaluate, observe, and recreate the very best version of yourself.
—Bianca G.

INSPIRATIONAL QUOTE
"Separation before elevation. You have to let some people and things go so you can go to the next level."

– Tony Gaskins

SUMMARY
Please write your demonstration of self-love today.

"Today, start your day with a smile, calmness of mind, coolness of emotions, and a heart filled with gratitude."
— Anonymous

Calmness | ˈkälmnəs | - the state of quality of being free from agitation in strong emotion.

POSITIVE AFFIRMATIONS
I feel light and calm.
I am at peace with myself and everything that surrounds me.

LESSON QUESTION
When are you in your calmest state of mind?

_____

_____

365 ON ME QUESTIONNAIRE
1. Is there a certain person, place, or thing that makes you feel calm?
    Yes
    No
    Undecided

REMINDER
When you're at your calmest, think of all things that bring you peace and joy. Rejoice in these times because you deserve it.
— Bianca G.

INSPIRATIONAL QUOTE
"Your strength is your calmness, in the clarity of your mind. Strength comes from putting the negative aside without reacting. Win in calmness, in consciousness, in balance."
— Yogi Amrit Desai

SUMMARY
Please write your demonstration of self-love today.

Life happens often, and we sometimes neglect the need to relax our mind, body, and soul. Today, focus on you, and relax as if there aren't other options.

— Bianca G.

Relaxation | ˌrē-ˌlak-ˈsā-shən | - the state of being free from tension and anxiety.

RELAXATION TECHNIQUES
- Deep breathing
- Meditation
- Music therapy
- Aromatherapy
- Yoga

LESSON QUESTION
What are some ways you choose to relax?

_____

_____

_____

365 ON ME QUESTIONNAIRE
1. Do I actually take the time to just relax?
   Yes
   No
   Undecided

REMINDER
It's vital that we learn to relax our minds for our mental health. Sometimes not going, not knowing, not saying, not doing and not being is all that needs to be.

—Bianca G.

INSPIRATIONAL QUOTE
"Relax, you are enough. You do enough. Breathe extra deep, let go, and just live right now in the moment."

— Unknown

SUMMARY
Please write your demonstration of self-love today.

_____

_____

_____

_____

_____

_____

_____

_____

_____

_____

_____

_____

_____

_____

_____

_____

_____

_____

"Eliminate all doubt and replace it with full expectation that you will receive what you are asking for."
— Unknown.

Manifestation | ˌma-nə-fə-ˈstā-shən | - an event, action, or object that clearly shows or embodies something, especially a theory or an abstract idea.

POSITIVE AFFIRMATION
Today, I will receive all that I deserve because I am speaking it, therefore, it is so.
—Bianca G.

LESSON QUESTION
What are some things you'd like to speak into existence?

_____

_____

_____

_____

_____

_____

365 ON ME QUESTIONNAIRE
1. Am I truly ready to receive all that I desire in this life?
   Yes
   No
   Undecided

REMINDER
"Ask for what you want, and be prepared to get it."
— Maya Angelou

INSPIRATIONAL QUOTE
"Destiny is not a matter of chance. It is a matter of choice.
— Unknown

SUMMARY
Please write your demonstration of self-love today.

Building self-assurance will demand new expectations of self, as well as viewing things from a different perspective. Set some goals, invest in a hobby, think of things that you're already good at, and identify new strengths and talents.

— Bianca G.

Self-assurance | ˌself-ə-ˈshu̇r-ən(t)s | - confidence in one's own abilities or character.

POSITIVE AFFIRMATION
I am confident in myself, and all that I desire to become in this life.
— Bianca G.

LESSON QUESTION
What are some things you desire for yourself that you're not quite sure you already possess?

_____

_____

_____

365 ON ME QUESTIONNAIRE
1. Do I seek validation from others, which is not allowing me to be certain of myself?
    Yes
    No
    Undecided

REMINDER
"Today, you are you! That is truer than true! There is no one alive who is you-er than you! Shout loud, I am lucky to be what I am!
— Dr. Suess

INSPIRATIONAL QUOTE
"When you recover or discover something that nourishes your soul and brings joy, care enough about yourself to make room for it in your life."
— Jean Shinoda Bolen

SUMMARY
Please write your demonstration of self-love today.

"Peace cannot be kept by force; it can only be achieved by understanding."

— Albert Einstein

Peace | ˈpēs | - freedom from disturbance; tranquility.

POSITIVE AFFIRMATIONS
I am still.
I am quiet.
I am peace.

— Bianca G.

LESSON QUESTION
What is your definition of peace?

_____

_____

365 ON ME QUESTIONNAIRE
1. Have I created peace in my life?
    Yes
    No
    Undecided

2. Would it take me letting go of certain things and people to experience peace in my life?
    Yes
    No
    Undecided

REMINDER
"You don't have to be positive all the time. It's perfectly okay to feel sad, angry, annoyed, frustrated, scared, and anxious. Having feelings doesn't make you a 'negative person.' It makes you human."

— Lori Deschene

INSPIRATIONAL QUOTE
"Nature is the best medicine for serenity. Peace, calmness, stillness. It's good for the heart."

– Karen Madewell

SUMMARY
Please write your demonstration of self-love today.

_____

_____

_____

_____

_____

_____

_____

_____

_____

_____

_____

_____

_____

_____

"Note to Self:
Healing is not an overnight process. It takes time. Sometimes, you'll feel like you are finally over something and happy again, and the wound will reopen. Don't give up; don't get discouraged. Take each day one step at a time. Just try to be in a better place mentally and emotionally than you were yesterday."
— *Unknown*

Healing | ˈhēl iŋ | - the process to make healthy, whole, or sound; to restore to health; to make free from ailment.

H - heal so that you may restore your peace and
E - embrace your scars so that you can
A - accrue self-love, understanding, peace and
L - love during the process.
— Bianca G.

LESSON QUESTION
What are some things that need healing in your life?

_____

_____

365 ON ME QUESTIONNAIRE
1. Do I need to heal from something or someone?
    Yes
    No
    Undecided

REMINDER
Healing is a process. Please understand that the soul is not in a rush, therefore allow yourself to feel every emotion, for this journey is preparing you for the unforeseen.
— Bianca G.

INSPIRATIONAL QUOTE
"The process of healing does not, and when the wounds are no longer visible. It ends when the wounds no longer ache."
—Unknown

SUMMARY
Please write your demonstration of self-love today."

_____

_____

_____

_____

_____

_____

_____

_____

_____

_____

_____

_____

_____

_____

_____

"Life challenges are not supposed to paralyze you; they're supposed to help you discover who you are."
— Bernice Johnson Reagon.

INSPIRATIONAL QUOTE
"Where there is no struggle, there is no strength."
— Oprah Winfrey

POSITIVE AFFIRMATION
Be comfortable, but be confident.
— Bianca G.

LESSON QUESTION
What are some things that bring you comfort?

_____

_____

_____

365 ON ME QUESTIONNAIRE
1. Am I comfortable with my level of confidence?
   Yes
   No
   Undecided

2. Have I become so relaxed and comfortable with my life that I no longer see room for growth?
   Yes
   No
   Undecided

REMINDER
Comfort comes with knowing and feeling courage and confidence. Do not mistake comfort with pleasure because pleasure is temporary, while comfort is growth.
— Bianca G.

INSPIRATIONAL QUOTE
"Step so far outside your comfort zone that you forget how to get back."
— Anonymous

SUMMARY
Please write your demonstration of self-love today.

_____

_____

_____

_____

_____

_____

_____

_____

_____

_____

_____

_____

_____

_____

_____

"Knowing when to walk away is wisdom. Being able to walk away is courage. Walking away with your head held high is dignity."

— Unknown

Dignity | ˈdig-nə-tē | - the state of quality of being worthy of honor or respect.

POSITIVE QUOTE
"Do not exchange your dignity for popularity."

— Dr. Steve Maraboli

LESSON QUESTIONS
What does dignity mean to you?

_____

_____

What does self-worth mean to you?

_____

_____

365 ON ME QUESTIONNAIRE
1. Are there things and/or people that I am allowing to impede my self confidence?
    Yes
    No
    Undecided

REMINDER
The way you treat others is a reflection of how you feel about yourself. So, be kind and gentle, but also be honest and real.

— Bianca G.

INSPIRATIONAL QUOTE

"Dignity. It means a belief in oneself, that one is worthy of the best. It means that what I have to say is important, and I will say it when it's important for me to say it. Dignity really means that I deserve the best treatment I can receive. And that I have the responsibility to give the best treatment I can to other people."
– Maya Angelou

SUMMARY

Please write your demonstration of self-love today.

_____

_____

_____

_____

_____

_____

_____

_____

_____

_____

_____

_____

_____

"To be yourself in the world that is constantly trying to make you something else is the greatest accomplishment."

— Emerson

POSITIVE AFFIRMATIONS
I am beautiful.
I am amazing.
I am ambitious.
I am me and there's no one else like me.

— Bianca G.

LESSON QUESTION
In your own words, what is the meaning of self-admiration?

_____

_____

365 ON ME QUESTIONNAIRE
1. Do I admire myself enough?
   Yes
   No
   Undecided

REMINDER
"Confidence is the ability to feel beautiful without needing someone to tell you."

— Unknown

INSPIRATIONAL QUOTE
"There is no passion to be found in settling for a life that is less than the one you are capable of living."

— Nelson Mandela

SUMMARY
Please write your demonstration of self-love today.

"Sometimes people are beautiful in looks. Not in what they say. Just in what they are.
— Mankus Zusak

Beauty | ˈbyü-tē | - the quality attributed to whatever pleases or satisfies the sense of mind, as by line, color, form, texture, proportion, rhythmic motion, tone etc; or by behavior, attitude, etc.

POSITIVE AFFIRMATION
I am beautiful today, tomorrow, and whenever, and however, I choose to be.
— Bianca G.

365 ON ME QUESTIONNAIRE
1. Have I embraced my inner beauty?
    Yes
    No
    Undecided

2. Have I acknowledged my outer beauty?
    Yes
    No
    Undecided

REMINDER
You define your meaning of beauty, so never allow anyone or anything to make you feel anything but, beautiful.
— Bianca G.

INSPIRATIONAL QUOTE
"Outer beauty attracts, but inner beauty captivates."
— Katie Angell

SUMMARY
Please write your demonstration of self-love today.

"If you have the courage to begin, you have the courage to succeed."

— Harry Hoover

Courage | ˈkər-ij | - the expression of boldness and confidence; the opposite of fear; strength in the face of adversity.

POSITIVE AFFIRMATIONS
Be bold.
Be courageous.
Be fierce.

— Bianca G.

LESSON QUESTION
What are some things that give you a sense of courage to accomplish a goal or complete a task?

_____

_____

_____

365 ON ME QUESTIONNAIRE
1. Am I bold in accomplishing personal goals?
   - Yes
   - No
   - Undecided

REMINDER
"I learned that courage is not the absence of fear, but the triumph over it. The brave man is not he who does not feel afraid, but he who confuses that fear.

— Nelson Mandela

INSPIRATIONAL QUOTE

"Courage is the most important of all the virtues, because without courage, you can't practice any virtue consistently."

— Maya Angelou

SUMMARY

Please write your demonstration of self-love today.

"Believe you can and you're halfway there."

– Theodore Roosevelt

Inspiration | ˌin(t)-spə-ˈrā-shən | - an inspiring agent of influence.

POSITIVE AFFIRMATIONS
Be amazing.
Be free.
Be inspiring—not only for others but for self.

– Bianca G.

LESSON QUESTION
What inspires me?

_____

_____

_____

365 ON ME QUESTIONNAIRE
1. Have I allowed myself to experience true self-inspiration?
    Yes
    No
    Undecided

REMINDER
- Write down the things that you admire.
- Focus on improvement but don't get distracted with trying to perfect your flaws.
- Accept responsibility for your actions.
- Now go out and conquer all that you set forth to do.

– Bianca G.

INSPIRATIONAL QUOTE
"I never lose. I either win or learn."

– Nelson Mandela

SUMMARY
Please write your demonstration of self-love today.

One who is determined will always show up whether scared, unprepared, or disheveled, but brave and eager to learn and grow. What counts is that you are present.
— Bianca G.

Determination | di-ˌtər-mə-ˈnā-shən | - firmness of purpose; resoluteness.

POSITIVE AFFIRMATIONS
I am successful, I am confident, I am powerful.
I am strong, I am an unstoppable force by nature.
— Unknown

LESSON QUESTION
What am I determined to accomplish in this life?

_____

_____

_____

365 ON ME QUESTIONNAIRE
1. Have I truly evaluated my ability to complete tasks I set forth?
    Yes
    No
    Undecided

REMINDER
Determination is getting up every day and doing what has to be done. Dedication is repeatedly doing what needs to be done. Consistency is continuously doing what must be done even when you don't feel motivated to get it done.
— Bianca G.

INSPIRATIONAL QUOTE
"Motivation gets you moving. Determination keeps you going."
— Unknown

SUMMARY
Please write your demonstration of self-love today.

"A hero is an ordinary individual who finds the strength to persevere and endure in spite of overwhelming obstacles."

— Christopher Reeve.

Perseverance | ˌpər-sə-ˈvir-ən(t)s | - the persistence in doing something despite difficulty or delay in achieving success.

POSITIVE AFFIRMATIONS
I am successful.
I am confident.
I am powerful.

— Bianca G.

LESSON QUESTION
What have you set forth in life that requires/required perseverance?

_____

_____

_____

365 ON ME QUESTIONNAIRE
1. Have I experienced persistence in the midst of a difficult task?
   Yes
   No
   Undecided

2. Are there obstacles that I have allowed to impede my ability to achieve something?
   Yes
   No
   Undecided

REMINDER
"It always seems impossible until it's done."

— Unknown

INSPIRATIONAL QUOTE

"The best versions of ourselves don't come out when everything is going amazing. The best versions of ourselves come out in the midst of trial, because that's where we grow. That's where our real substance comes out. That's where you find the person you were always meant to be; the person who was there all along."

– Ashley Hetherington

SUMMARY

Please write your demonstration of self-love today.

_____
_____
_____
_____
_____
_____
_____
_____
_____
_____
_____
_____
_____
_____

The power of understanding adds value to one's life. We are able to perceive vital information, which is stored in memory for access.

– Bianca G.

Understanding | ˌən-dər-ˈstan-diŋ | - to perceive the intended meaning of words, a language, or a speaker.

POSITIVE QUOTE
"To understand and to be understood makes our happiness on earth. Understanding comes through communication, and through understanding, we find the way to peace. To understand and to be understood makes our happiness on earth."
– Unknown

LESSON QUESTION
What is it that you seek to understand?

_____

_____

_____

_____

365 ON ME QUESTIONNAIRE
1. Are you able to perceive information that is a vital aspect of your life?
    Yes
    No
    Undecided

REMINDER
Seek understanding through listening quietly, not listening only to respond.
– Bianca G.

INSPIRATIONAL QUOTE

"Understanding is deeper than knowledge. There are many people who you know, but very few who understand you."

– Nicolas Cage

SUMMARY

Please write your demonstration of self-love today.

_____
_____
_____
_____
_____
_____
_____
_____
_____
_____
_____
_____
_____
_____
_____

"An individual's self-concept is the core of his personality. It affects every aspect of human behavior: the ability to learn, the capacity to grow and change. A strong, positive self-image is the best possible preparation for success in life.

— Unknown

Self-concept | ˈself-ˈkän-ˌsept | - a confidencxxx.

POSITIVE AFFIRMATIONS
I am a kind person.
I am a good friend.

— Bianca G.

365 ON ME QUESTIONNAIRE
1. Do my beliefs about who I am positively impact my ability to be creative and unique?
   Yes
   No
   Undecided

2. Are there personal beliefs that impact my ability to grow?
   Yes
   No
   Undecided

REMINDER
"Your self-concept is determined by a collection of beliefs about you. Choose what is real and true to your soul. Eliminate every thought of doubt, and feed your mind with consistent motivation and positive attitudes and behaviors."

— Bianca G.

SUMMARY
Please write your demonstration of self-love today.

"A smart person knows what to say. A wise person knows whether or not to say it."

– Unknown

Wisdom | ˈwiz-dəm | - the quality of having experience, knowledge, and good judgment; the quality of being wise.

Write a positive word for each letter of wisdom.

W - _____

I - _____

S - _____

D - _____

O - _____

M - _____

LESSON QUESTION
Name five wise choices you've made over the past six weeks.

1. _____

2. _____

3. _____

4. _____

5. _____

365 ON ME QUESTIONNAIRE
1. Am I allowing myself to experience more in life that could enhance my knowledge?
   Yes
   No
   Undecided

According to a source, there are eight pieces of wisdom that can change your life:
1. Words are powerful; use them wisely.
2. People come and go, but the right ones stay.
3. You are doing enough even if it doesn't feel like it.
4. Failure is when you don't try.
5. Random acts of kindness make everyone feel better.
6. Live for today, not for tomorrow.
7. Never look back; there is nothing there for you.
8. Overthinking kills happiness.

— Unknown

REMINDER

To know is to understand. To believe is to feel. To acknowledge is to be aware. Therefore, wisdom is all of the above.

— Bianca G.

SUMMARY

Please write your demonstration of self-love today.

_____

_____

_____

_____

_____

_____

_____

_____

"Whether you think you can or you think you can't, you are right."
— Unknown

Knowledge | ˈnä-lij | - the facts, information, and skills acquired through experience or education; the theoretical or practical understanding of a subject.

THE FAMOUS QUOTE
"Knowledge is powerful."
— Unknown

LESSON QUESTION
What does this quote mean to you?

_____

_____

365 ON ME QUESTIONNAIRE
1. Do I possess the knowledge to make the necessary changes in my life?
    Yes
    No
    Undecided

2. Will changing my mind affect the way that I think and understand others?
    Yes
    No
    Undecided

REMINDER
"I alone cannot change the world, but I can cast a stone across the water to create many ripples."
— Unknown

INSPIRATIONAL QUOTE
"Knowledge is a commodity for knowledge to pay dividends. It should not remain the monopoly of the selected few."
— Unknown

SUMMARY
Please write your demonstration of self-love today.

"The more you take responsibility for your past and present, the more you are able to create the future you seek."
— Unknown

Responsibility |ri-ˌspän(t)-sə-ˈbi-lə-tē| - the state of fact of having a duty to deal with something or having control over someone.

LESSON QUESTION
What new responsibilities have you adopted?

_____

_____

_____

_____

365 ON ME QUESTIONNAIRE
1. Have you avoided some responsibilities due to being afraid of the outcome?
    Yes
    No
    Undecided

2. Are you open to adopting new responsibilities to meet your goals?
    Yes
    No
    Undecided

REMINDER
"With great power comes great responsibility."
— Unknown

INSPIRATIONAL QUOTE
"Responsibility is accepting that you are the cause and the solution of the matter."
— Unknown

SUMMARY
Please write your demonstration of self-love today.

"Everything begins inside your mind, with the right mind that you will succeed."
— Unknown

Mindset | ˈmīn(d)-ˌset | - the establishment of an attitude held by someone.

THREE KINDS OF MINDSETS
- Abundance – belief that there are enough resources in the world for eveyone.
- Positive – optimistic about the world around you.
- Growth – dedication and hard work.

Write the meaning of abundance, positive, and growth mindset.

_____

_____

_____

_____

365 ON ME QUESTIONNAIRE
1. Is there a lack of abundance, positivity, and growth mindset in my life?
   Yes
   No
   Undecided

REMINDER
"If you believe, you can learn what it takes to create your success at work and in life. Congratulations! You have a growth mindset."
— Unknown

INSPIRATIONAL QUOTE
"Stop limiting yourself. Change your mindset from "I can't" to "How can I?"
— Unknown

SUMMARY
Please write your demonstration of self-love today.

"It is not only what we do, but also what we do not do, for which we are accountable."
— Moliere

Accountability | ə-ˌkaun-tə-ˈbi-lə-tē | - the fact or condition of being accountable; responsibility.

PERSONAL ACCOUNTABILITY ASK
How did I:
- Add value (ex. improvements made)
- Identify and correct my mistakes (ex. called myself out for a mishap)
- Take ownership (ex. accountability, responsibility and acknowledgment of my choices)
- Have a positive mindset (ex. moving forward I can make healthier decisions)
- Make responsible choices (ex. do things that I can live with the results)

LESSON QUESTION
What are some things and/or situations I hold myself accountable for?

_____

_____

_____

_____

365 ON ME QUESTIONNAIRE
1. Am I responsible for my happiness?
   Yes
   No
   Undecided

REMINDER
"The choices we make are ultimately our responsibility."
— Unknown

INSPIRATIONAL QUOTE
"Without personal accountability, we cannot grow, nor can we ever improve ourselves."
– Unknown

SUMMARY
Please write your demonstration of self-love today.

_____

_____

_____

_____

_____

_____

_____

_____

_____

_____

_____

_____

_____

_____

_____

"Your self-realization is the greatest service you can render the world."

– Ramana Maharishi

Realization | ˌrē-ə-lə-ˈzā-shən | - an act of becoming fully aware of something as a fact.

POSITIVE AFFIRMATIONS
I am aware.
I know better.
I will get it.

– Bianca G.

LESSON QUESTION
What skill or achievement have I desired but have yet to make a reality in my life?

_____

_____

_____

365 ON ME QUESTIONNAIRE
1. Am I aware of my strengths?
    Yes
    No
    Undecided

2. Will I take the necessary steps to identify the abilities that I have ignored in the past?
    Yes
    No
    Undecided

REMINDER
Self-realization helps us to not only know who we are, but what we have the ability to become.

– Bianca G.

INSPIRATIONAL QUOTE
"Realization is a matter of becoming conscious of that which is already realized."
– Wei Wu Wei

SUMMARY
Please write your demonstration of self-love today.

Learning yourself is an ongoing task that you will have to continue experiencing.
— Bianca G.

10 Signs You're an Empath
1. You feel the emotions of others.
2. You take on the energy of others.
3. When others are happy, you are happy.
4. You are easily drained by negative people.
5. Strangers ask you for advice.
6. Your intuition is accurate.
7. You feel drawn to help others.
8. The weather affects your mood.
9. You can feel things before they happen.
10. You listen to people's energy, not words.
— Unknown

Empath | ˈem-ˌpath | - the ability to understand and share the feelings of another.

LESSON QUESTIONS

Are you an empath?
_____

If so, what do you desire to experience more of with this ability?
_____
_____
_____

REMINDER

Feeling what another is feeling can be very powerful, yet draining at times. Learn to balance your thoughts, feelings, and actions to ensure that you have enough fuel to sustain yourself.
— Bianca G.

INSPIRATIONAL QUOTE

"As empaths, we are not here to be sponges or enable. We are here to be helpers, guides, and supporters."

– Aletheia Luna

SUMMARY

Please write your demonstration of self-love today.

_____
_____
_____
_____
_____
_____
_____
_____
_____
_____
_____
_____
_____
_____

It is in my mind, my body, and my soul that I am well.

— Bianca G.

Wellness | ˈwel-nəs | - the state of being in good health, especially as an actively pursued goal.

The six dimensions of wellness include physical, mental, spiritual, social, environmental, and emotional. Provide an act or practice of healthy habits that you engage in daily and/or would like to attain better outcomes in.

Physical – _____

Mental – _____

Spiritual – _____

Social – _____

Environmental – _____

Emotional – _____

LESSON QUESTION
How can I improve my spiritual wellness?

_____

_____

_____

365 ON ME QUESTIONNAIRE
1. Are there areas of my life that require wellness protection?
   Yes
   No
   Undecided

REMINDER
Being well in every aspect of your life creates positive interactions and experiences with not only others, but with yourself.

— Bianca G.

INSPIRATIONAL QUOTE
"I release stress in my body with every exhaled breath."
— Unknown

SUMMARY
Please write your demonstration of self-love today.

_____

_____

_____

_____

_____

_____

_____

_____

_____

_____

_____

_____

_____

_____

_____

_____

"I am worthy of all the things I want. I believe in myself and my ability to reach my goals. I am surrounded by positive people who help me achieve my goals. I attract amazing opportunities and abundance every day."

— Unknown

Purpose | ˈpər-pəs | - the reason for which something is done or created or for which something exists.

In your own words, what is the meaning of purpose?

_____

_____

Complete sentences using your purpose-driven life.
   Fly beautiful butterfly, just fly. There is nothing that can _____ me.
   I am _____ and my strength comes from _____.
   I am capable of _____ because of my _____
   to demonstrate _____.
   — Bianca and _____

POSITIVE AFFIRMATIONS
I wake up every day rising with a clear mind, clean slate, and connection to my life purpose.
I am true to myself.
I am conscious of my time and my life.
I matter.

— Bianca G.

365 ON ME QUESTIONNAIRE
1. Have I identified my purpose prior to this assignment?
    Yes
    No
    Undecided

2. Do I believe that I possess all that's needed to live at my purpose in this life?
    Yes
    No
    Undecided

REMINDER
Only you define your purpose in this life. Do not allow an author or illustrator to write your story or define for you what it means to be purposeful.
— Bianca G.

INSPIRATIONAL QUOTE
"I am in control of how I live my life. I am allowed to take my path. I put energy into the things that matter to me. I am free to create the life desire. I am capable of making my decisions."
— Unknown

SUMMARY
Please write your demonstration of self-love today.

_____

_____

_____

_____

_____

_____

_____

_____

_____

_____

_____

"You learn at your best when you have something you care about and can get pleasure from being engaged in."

– Howard Gardner

Self-educated | ˌself-ˈe-jə-ˌkā-təd | - to be educated largely through one's own efforts, rather than by formal instructions.

List five ways you can become self-educated (ex. reading, exploring, traveling, and asking questions).

1. _____
2. _____
3. _____
4. _____
5. _____

LESSON QUESTION
What does it mean to be self-educated?

_____

_____

_____

Write three areas of your life in which you can contribute to your self-education. (ex. spiritual, relationships, and friendships).

1. _____
2. _____
3. _____

REMINDER
"Formal education will make you a living; self-education will make you a fortune."
– Jim Rohn

INSPIRATIONAL QUOTE
"The goal of education is the advancement of knowledge and the discrimination of truth."

– John Fitzgerald Kennedy

SUMMARY
Please write your demonstration of self-love today.

___
___
___
___
___
___
___
___
___
___
___
___
___
___
___

Be bold, be courageous, be unforgettable, be determined, and be you. Besides, there's no one else quite like you.
— Bianca G.

Boldness | ˈbōld | - the willingness to take risks and act innovatively; confidence or courage.

Create your
(examples)
B - Bravery triumphs fear   **B** –
O – Opportunity outweighs   **O** –
L – Losses and   **L** –
D – Determination is key   **D** –

LESSON QUESTION
What makes you bold?

_____

_____

365 ON ME QUESTIONNAIRE
1. Have you identified areas of your life that require you to be bold?
   Yes
   No
   Undecided

2. Are there obstacles or fears that distract you from being bold?
   Yes
   No
   Undecided

REMINDER
"Be bold. Be brave enough to be your true self."
— Queen Latifah

INSPIRATIONAL QUOTE
"A tiger doesn't lose sleep over the opinion of sheep."
— Shahir Zag

SUMMARY
Please write your demonstration of self-love today.

Living in a world where everyone judges doesn't exclude you or me. Become the most influential judge of yourself so that you can critique, recreate, and reinvent the best version of yourself.
— Bianca G.

Evaluation | i-ˌval-yə-ˈwā-shən | - an idea of the self constructed from the beliefs one holds about oneself and the responses of others.

ASSESSMENT

Let's pretend today is self-evaluation day. Ranging from one to five (with one being the least and five being the most), evaluate yourself in each area listed below and provide a plan to enhance self-evaluation next to it.

Open-mindedness Rate (1-5)____ _____

Persistence Rate (1-5)____ _____

Accountability Rate (1-5)____ _____

Self-discipline Rate (1-5)____ _____

365 ON ME QUESTIONNAIRE

1. Have you purposely ignored self-evaluation due to fear or self-doubt?
    Yes
    No
    Undecided

2. Are you allowing past failures to prevent you from critical judgment of yourself?
    Yes
    No
    Undecided

REMINDER

"Continuous improvement is better than delayed perfection."
— Mark Twain

INSPIRATIONAL QUOTE

"Ask yourself if what you're doing today is getting you closer to where you want to be tomorrow."

– Unknown

SUMMARY

Please write your demonstration of self-love today.

_____

_____

_____

_____

_____

_____

_____

_____

_____

_____

_____

_____

_____

_____

"Self-discovery is the best investment that you can make."

— Michele Scholz-Evers

Discovery | di-ˈskə-v(ə-)rē | - the action or process or discovering or being discovered.

Read and complete by filling in the blank spaces.

Dear Me,
There are so many places to go and things to see to discover me.
Where there is opportunity, I will _____ and _____ .
Through my vision of _____ , I am strong,
beautiful _____ optimistic, _____ because
it is _____ .

LESSON QUESTION

1. Thinking about the characteristics that make you who you are, what else will it take for you to execute your goals?

   _____

   _____

2. Have you been sleeping on who you are because of self-doubt or fear? No more sleeping! Write down five of your characteristics and create a small execution plan to discover who you are based on the characteristics you possess.

   1. _____
   2. _____
   3. _____
   4. _____
   5. _____

Execution plan:

_____

_____

_____

_____

REMINDER
Repeat daily affirmations that speak volumes to your soul.

INSPIRATIONAL QUOTE
"He who never made a mistake never made a discovery."
— Samuel Smiles

SUMMARY
Please write your demonstration of self-love today.

_____

_____

_____

_____

_____

_____

_____

_____

_____

_____

_____

_____

"The only difference between a good day and a bad day is your attitude."

— Dennis Brown

Attitude | ˈa-tə-ˌtüd | - a settled way of thinking or feeling about someone or something, typically one that is reflected in a person's behavior.

Define your attitude about your life.

_____

_____

Circle all affirmations that you'd want to quote daily.

My challenges help me grow.	I can control my happiness.
I forgive myself for my mistakes.	I give myself permission to make choices.
Today, I choose to think positively.	I have courage and confidence.

Now, write six of your daily affirmations you plan to speak about every day.

_____

_____

_____

_____

_____

_____

LESSON QUESTION

What is an example of your positive attitude?

_____

_____

_____

REMINDER
You are only as great as you think you are, and if you do not think you are great, change your mind so that you can change your life.

INSPIRATIONAL QUOTE
"Our attitude towards life determines life's attitude towards us."

— John Mitchell

SUMMARY
Please write your demonstration of self-love today.

_____

_____

_____

_____

_____

_____

_____

_____

_____

_____

_____

_____

Daily deposits of positive thinking, loving on yourself, and recognizing your abilities will be the fruit of your labor, and your labor, my dear, is your self-investment.

– Bianca G.

Investment | in-ˈves(t)-mənt | - the action or process of investing for profit or material result.

According to Bianca, self-investment is the unmatched effort and consistency of putting in good work on yourself, and in return, you will witness the growth and development of self-made majesty.

Please write your definition of self-investment.

_____

_____

LESSON QUESTION

1. Name two self-investments you have made deposits in.

   _____   _____

2. What areas of your life lack self-investment?(i.e. self-love, finances, motivation)

   _____

   _____

3. In the next 30 days, focus on investing more of your time in these areas.

   (1) _____

   (2) _____

   (3) _____

REMINDER

"Speed is the currency that you want to maximize on today. Most people go too slow. They think too long, and they never take action."

– Grant Cardone

INSPIRATIONAL QUOTE
The very moment you realize there's more to be done is the very moment you have to do it. Investment requires action; action from self will produce results that will continue to improve per deposit.

— Bianca G.

SUMMARY
Please write your demonstration of self-love today.

"Believe in your infinite potential. Your only limitations are those you set upon yourself."

– Roy T. Bennett

Potential | pə-'ten(t)-shəl | - having or showing the capability to become or develop into something in the future.

Identify, match, and start to develop your potential. (Draw lines from the left side items to match the items on the right side.)

A. Determination

- I will identify what is required for me to be successful and not allow difficulties to distract me. I am steadfast.

B. Achievement

- I acknowledge my abilities, and now, I'll get to work.

C. Perseverance

- I have decided that I will put in the work until I am satisfied with the result.

D. Capability

- I have potential because I believe in all that I can do.

E. Recognition

- I will celebrate all that I have accomplished. I deserve to be honored.

Now that you're on your journey to embrace all that you are capable of doing and being, write here a short dedication letter to yourself. From this day forward, you will reflect on this letter as a gentle reminder to keep going. Go, you!

Dear me,

_____

_____

_____

_____

365 ON ME QUESTIONNAIRE

1. Have you unintentionally ignored your potential due to being overwhelmed with other personal obligations?

    Yes
    No
    Undecided

REMINDER

You're only as capable as you believe you are.

— Bianca G.

INSPIRATIONAL QUOTE

"If you want happiness, fulfillment, success, and inner peace, start thinking you have the power to achieve those things."

— Unknown

SUMMARY

Please write your demonstration of self-love today.

_____

_____

_____

_____

_____

_____

_____

_____

"Your journey will be much lighter and easier if you don't carry your past with you."
— Unknown

Renew | ri-'nü | - to resume after an interruption.

Words that come to mind when you are in the process of renewal:
- Resume
- Extend
- Continue
- Allow
- Refresh
- Go Forth

From the six above-identified words that are derived from renew, think about where you are right now in life. Identify specific areas that require renewed strength, and complete an inspirational quote using all six words.

Example of an inspirational quote: "Go forth in life and allow yourself to hit the refresh button. Even when and if you feel you can't continue, extend yourself grace and resume the task you are destined to complete."
— Bianca G.

_____

_____

_____

LESSON QUESTION

Identify two areas of your life that require a renewal.
_____   _____

Are these areas personal or professional? _____

Create a self-contract for renewal of the identified personal/professional areas identified above. Fill in the blanks.

Today's Date:
I, _____ , abide by the terms of this self-renewal contract. And I vow to excel in these/this area(s) _____ on both good and bad days. I will give myself daily encouragement and _____ .
I vow to _____ whole-heartedly.

Signed: _____

REMINDER
"When I let go of what I am, I become what I might be."
— Lao Tzo

INSPIRATIONAL QUOTE
"I open my hands to the gifts of change. I let nature teach me the passion of letting go in order to make way for renewal."
— Unknown

SUMMARY
Please write your demonstration of self-love today.

_____
_____
_____
_____
_____
_____
_____
_____
_____
_____
_____
_____

"I am in charge of how I feel, and today, I feel fierce."
— Unknown

Fierce | ˈfirs | - having or displaying an intense or ferocious aggressiveness.

In your own words, what is the meaning of fierce?
_____
_____

5 POSITIVE FIERCE AFFIRMATIONS
- I am strong.
- I am powerful.
- I am confident.
- I am an unstoppable force of nature.
- I am successful.

— Bianca G.

Create five of your own fierce affirmations.

1. _____
2. _____
3. _____
4. _____
5. _____

365 ON ME QUESTIONNAIRE

1. Do I have what it requires to demonstrate my fierce abilities?
    Yes
    No
    Undecided

2. Am I allowing certain people or situations to distract me from my fierce abilities?
    Yes
    No
    Undecided

REMINDER
There is a fire inside of you. Sometimes in order to experience the flames, you must first get the fire started.
— Bianca G.

INSPIRATIONAL QUOTE
"He is fierce like a lion, yet humble in his demeanor."
— Unknown

SUMMARY
Please write your demonstration of self-love today.

_____

_____

_____

_____

_____

_____

_____

_____

_____

_____

_____

_____

"A moment's insight is sometimes with a life's experience."

— Oliver Wendell Holmes Sr.

Insight | ˈin-ˌsīt | - an instance of apprehending the true nature of a thing, especially through intuitive understanding. (2) An understanding of the motivational forces behind one's actions, thoughts, or behavior; self-knowledge.

Take a moment to think about something you have inquired about and/or that has piqued your interest. Write a short paragraph about your insight into the world we live in. For instance, think about all the things you admire, accept, believe, and/or would like to make a positive change to within this world.

_____
_____
_____
_____
_____
_____

ADVICE FROM A TREE
- Stand tall and proud.
- Go out on a limb.
- Remember your roots.
- Drink plenty of water.
- Be content with your natural beauty.
- Enjoy the view.

— Unknown

LESSON QUESTION
What insight do you have regarding your life?

_____
_____

365 ON ME QUESTIONNAIRE

1. Have you allowed yourself to think about the lifestyle you'd like to create for yourself?
   - Yes
   - No
   - Undecided

2. Are you taking steps to create insightful life experiences?
   - Yes
   - No
   - Undecided

REMINDER

"It is never too late to be who you might have been."

— George Elliot

INSPIRATIONAL QUOTE

"For those with insight, life is an upward path."

— Unknown

SUMMARY

Please write your demonstration of self-love today.

_____

_____

_____

_____

_____

_____

Darling, it's time to preserve your energy for the things you actually need. Sometimes, that means ending things so that you are well enough to experience great things.

– Bianca G.

Energy | ˈe-nər-jē | - the strength and vitality required for sustained physical or mental activity.

LESSON QUESTIONS

What are three things/substances you have allowed to absorb your energy? (ex: relationship, work, etc.)

_____

_____

_____

Where do you spend most of your energy in life? (ex: work, family, relationship, education)

_____

_____

What are five new sources you'd like to start investing your time and attention? (ex: self-care, relationship, solitude, education, etc)

_____

_____

_____

_____

_____

365 ON ME QUESTIONNAIRE

1. Are there specific areas in your life that you'd like to engage more time and focus in?
    Yes
    No
    Undecided

REMINDER
"The more positive energy you throw into the universe, the more positive energy it gives you back."

— Nitin Namdeo

INSPIRATIONAL QUOTE
"What you think, you become. What you feel, you attract. What you imagine, you create."

— Buddha

SUMMARY
Please write your demonstration of self-love today.

_____

_____

_____

_____

_____

_____

_____

_____

_____

_____

_____

_____

As high as the sky, as wide as the universe, and as free as you can be, spread your wings and fly high, bird. Fly high.

— Bianca G.

Ambition |am-ˈbi-shən| - a strong desire to do or achieve something, typically requiring determination and hard work.

    A – achieve
    M – magnificent things in life and be
    B – brave, knowing that you are walking into the most
    I – impeccable moments of this life with
    T – transcendent experiences and
    I – independence
    O – optimistic mindset for a
    N – nonpareil being which you are becoming.

Create your breakdown of ambition as the provided example above:

A – _____
M – _____
B – _____
I – _____
T – _____
I – _____
O – _____
N – _____

LESSON QUESTIONS
What makes you feel ambitious?

_____
_____
_____
_____

Name five inspirational experiences that would motivate you to feel ambitious about completing important tasks.

1. _____
2. _____
3. _____
4. _____
5. _____

REMINDER
"Don't be afraid to be ambitious about your goals. Hard work never stops. Neither should your dreams."

— Dwayne Johnson

INSPIRATIONAL QUOTE
"To me, if I can bring one second of joy into a child's or a grown-up's life, then I have achieved my lifetime ambition."

— Michael Jackson

SUMMARY
Please write your demonstration of self-love today.

_____
_____
_____
_____
_____
_____
_____

"The thing about meditation is: You become more and more you."

— David Lynch

Meditation | ˌme-də-ˈtā-shən | - the action or practice of meditating.

MEDITATION AFFIRMATIONS

I am peaceful.
I am calm.
I am present.
I am happy.
My meditation practice is getting better by the day.
I can find time for myself and my needs.
All my thoughts are okay.
My life is going well.

— Unknown

Out of the eight meditation affirmations above, select four that you believe you feel. Identify four that you'd like to embrace in order to enhance your mindset.

1. _____

2. _____

3. _____

4. _____

365 ON ME QUESTIONNAIRE

1. Do you practice meditation? If so, do you practice often?
    Yes
    No
    Undecided

2. Are your thoughts of meditation conflicting with your current prayer life?
    Yes
    No
    Undecided

REMINDER
The ability to sit in silence while in solitude allows you a great skill that continuously enhances your strength and focuses in the moment, that lasts a lifetime.
— Bianca G.

INSPIRATIONAL QUOTE
"Meditation is a way for nourishing and blossoming the divinity within you."
— Amit Ray

SUMMARY
Please write your demonstration of self-love today.

_____

_____

_____

_____

_____

_____

_____

_____

_____

_____

_____

_____

"The function of education is to teach one to think intensively and to think critically. Intelligence plus character—that is the goal of true education."

— Martin Luther King Jr.

Critical thinking | ˈkri-ti-kəl thiŋ-kiŋ | - the objective analysis and education of an issue in order to form a judgment.

Circle each situation that you believe requires critical thinking.

- Starting a new job
- Making a salad or tuna sandwich
- Quitting a job
- Taking a nap
- Reading a book
- Dating after a divorce
- Meeting your child's teacher
- Doing yoga
- Continuing an abusive relationship
- Communicating effectively to gain a better understanding

LESSON QUESTIONS

What are three situations in which you have used critical thinking?

_____

_____

_____

_____

_____

_____

Has there been circumstances in your life where you should've used critical thinking, but didn't? If so, name at least two and identify new education you would apply moving forward.

_____

_____

_____

_____

365 ON ME QUESTIONNAIRE

1. Have you neglected important situations by not applying critical thinking when you knew it was needed?

    Yes
    No
    Undecided

REMINDER

"When your mind is full of assumptions, conclusions, and beliefs, it has no penetration, it just repeats past impressions."

    – Sadhguru

INSPIRATIONAL QUOTES

"Education is our passport to the future for tomorrow belongs to the people who prepare for it today."

    – Malcolm X

"Literary education is of no value if it is not able to build up a sound character."

    – Mahatma Gandhi

"The inspirational value of the space program is probably of far greater importance to education than any input of dollars... A whole generation is growing up which has been attached to the hard disciplines of science and engineering by the romance of space."

    – Arthur C. Clarke

SUMMARY

Please write your demonstration of self-love today.

_____

_____

_____

_____

_____

"We have a responsibility to influence the people in our lives to be the best possible people they can be. Therefore encourage one another and build each other up."

— Henry Cloud John Townsend

"Although I truly, truly admire the above inspirational message, I'd like to create one that speaks to individuality. Here goes: It is my responsibility to be the force of influence to myself and for myself by being the epitome of an unparalleled mirror reflection of myself. Therefore, I speak motivation, life, peace, and positivity over my life."

— Bianca G.

Influence | ˈin-ˌflü-ən(t)s | - the capacity to have an effect on the character, development, or behavior of someone or something, or the effect itself.

LESSON QUESTIONS

What influences you to be the best person that you can be?

___

___

Who influences you to be the best person that you can be?

___

___

What areas in your life require more motivational influences to complete tasks?

___

___

In what ways, positively or negatively, have two specific people influenced and/or impacted your life?

___

___

What negative choices have you made due to the negative influences of others?

___

___

REMINDER
"As much as people refuse to believe it, the company you keep does have an impact and influence on your choices."

— Unknown

INSPIRATIONAL QUOTES
"Nothing is impossible."

"Keep your face always towards the sunshine, and shadows will fall behind you."

"There is nothing impossible to those who will try."

— Unknown

SUMMARY
Please write your demonstration of self-love today.

_____
_____
_____
_____
_____
_____
_____
_____
_____
_____
_____

"There comes a time in life when we need to reevaluate aspects of our life. In these times, we will identify things, people, and circumstances that do not align with our spirit. It is during this time that change is warranted."

— Bianca G.

PERSONAL SHARE FROM THE AUTHOR

There came a specific time in my life (July 25, 2021) when I realized just how serious it was for me to go into complete solitude. I was hospitalized with COVID-19 and severe pneumonia. Now, I'm not the one to share with the world most of my personal and intimate experiences, especially illness; however, I will give you a glimpse of my reality for educational and inspirational purposes during my 16 days hospital stay. Over half of the time, I received negative reporting from the doctors and nurses. I was drained physically because the virus had taken a toll on my breathing to the point that I could barely speak a complete sentence without pausing to catch my breath. And honestly, my lungs were screaming for no added force to communicate, so I didn't say much to many. I slowly began to decline emotionally, mentally, and spiritually. I was devastated by my circumstances, and negativity started to creep in. My son and sister were the only two individuals I cared to communicate with daily. They both offered me inspiration, support, and, most of all, their extended love for me. I thought, How can I (the strong one) allow this temporary situation to dictate the rest of my life? I started to reevaluate certain people and circumstances in my life, and it hit me all of a sudden: The universe is speaking to me loudly (COVID, hospitalization, other significant instances I experienced), and I'm so focused on my impairment that I'm missing out on an opportunity. Although I was "forced" into solitude, those 16 lonely days in that hospital changed my life forever! I reevaluated every area (relationships, education, finances, spirituality, friendships, etc.) of my life that I could think of, and my healing started immediately. I had at least another week in the hospital; however, I became spiritually strong by speaking strength, love, motivation, and peace over my life. I discharged myself on day 16!

— Bianca G.

Write your story regarding a moment in your life when you reevaluated something.

_____

_____

_____

_____

Reevaluate | (ˌ)rē-i-ˈval-yə-ˌwāt | - to evaluate again or differently.

LESSON QUESTION
Identify three significant situations, things, circumstances, and/or persons that requires reevaluation pertaining to your life.

_____

_____

_____

_____

Now list one important change you will apply for each instance.

_____

_____

_____

_____

REMINDER
Reevaluation of one's life is personal, and it offers growth and wisdom when you can identify, confront, and change all that doesn't welcome peace in your life.
— Bianca G.

INSPIRATIONAL QUOTES
"Sometimes, we have to reevaluate ourselves, our circle, or our plan of action, and then make tough decisions."
— Royale le Braain

"Evaluate the people in your life; then promote, demote, or terminate. You're the CEO of your life."
— Unknown

SUMMARY
Please write your demonstration of self-love today.

"Fill your life with experiences, not things. Have stories to tell, not stuff to show."
— Unknown

Explore | ik-'splór | - to travel in or through in order to learn about or familiarize oneself with it.

PERSONAL SHARE FROM THE AUTHOR

Go into the world, explore, learn, be adventurous, and live. As of this very point in writing this workbook, I'm currently in St. Thomas, The Virgin Islands on my continued 15-day vacation, arriving from Santorini, Greece only a few days ago. Live your life, my friend, and travel the world to see and experience beautiful things in life. Travel is educational.
— Bianca G.

LESSON QUESTION

Are there some things that you feel prevent you from traveling? If so, list them here.

_____

_____

List five places in this world you'd like to visit.

_____   _____   _____

_____   _____

Considering the places you named above, let's execute a plan for you to start exploring. Fill in this self-care commitment note to yourself:

Today, I pledge to engage in self-care by exploring the world through travels. I will not allow _____ to hinder or discourage me. Instead, I feel _____ and _____ when I _____ about living my best life through traveling the world. I will work on _____ so that I can and go!

— Sincerely me, _____

REMINDER
Anything in this life that you want to do, do it! Whatever desires you have on your heart, go out and experience life, and you will find that you will never return the same.
— Bianca G.

INSPIRATIONAL QUOTE
"Bound by no boundaries, contained by no countries, tamed by no time, she is the force of nature's course."
— Roman Payne

SUMMARY
Please write your demonstration of self-love today.

_____
_____
_____
_____
_____
_____
_____
_____
_____
_____
_____
_____

"Being self-made is a state of mind, and once you put that mentality to work, your success will come."

– Dave East

Mentality | men-ˈta-lə-tē | - the characteristic attitude of mind or way of thinking of a person or group.

In your own words, what is the meaning of mentality?
_____
_____

LESSON QUESTIONS
What are some positive thoughts that can challenge your reality?
_____
_____
_____

What is the difference between a positive mindset and a negative mindset?
_____
_____
_____

365 ON ME QUESTIONNAIRE
1. Have I allowed a negative mindset to distract me from getting things done?
   Yes
   No
   Undecided

2. Does the way you think determine your decisions in life?
   Yes
   No
   Undecided

REMINDER
Change your mind. Change your life.
— Bianca G.

INSPIRATIONAL QUOTE
"We don't cower, we don't run. We endure and conquer."
— Kobe Bryant

SUMMARY
Please write your demonstration of self-love today.

_____

_____

_____

_____

_____

_____

_____

_____

_____

_____

_____

_____

_____

"Belief in oneself is one of the most important bricks in building any successful venture."
– Lydia M. Child

Venture | ˈven(t)-shər | - a risky or daring journey or undertaking.

V – vacations offer versatility and visionary
E – experiences that last a lifetime and these moments are
N – nonpareil
T – top-notch
U – unique
R – rewarding and remarkably
E – educational

Fill in the blanks
I want to challenge myself to take a vacation to _____
During this time, I will fully _____ and
_____ so that I can truly experience
_____ while allowing this challenge of venturing to _____.

LESSON QUESTIONS
What are the two most challenging thoughts that come to your mind when you think about venturing?
_____
_____
_____

Where would you like your first new venture to be?
_____

REMINDER
Go out into the world, live, and explore. There's so much to see and do. Become fully engaged with your challenge, and before you know it, it's no longer challenging.
– Bianca G.

INSPIRATIONAL QUOTE

"That's the beauty of starting lines: Until you begin a new venture, you never know what awaits you."

— Amby Burfoot

SUMMARY

Please write your demonstration of self-love today.

_____
_____
_____
_____
_____
_____
_____
_____
_____
_____
_____
_____
_____
_____
_____

"You have the power within you to overcome every situation. It is all in your mind: if you can conceive it, you shall receive it."

– Setjhaba Msibi

Power | ˈpau̇(-ə)r | - the ability to do something or act in a particular way, especially as a faculty or quality.

LESSON QUESTIONS

What does possessing power mean to you?
_____
_____

How often do you recognize when you use your powers?
_____
_____

What area in your life would you like to enhance your ability to be in control of?
_____
_____

365 ON ME QUESTIONNAIRE

1. Have you disregarded your ability to use your powers due to others not approving?
    Yes
    No
    Undecided

REMINDER

"With great power comes great responsibility."

– Peter Parker (Spider Man)

INSPIRATIONAL QUOTE
"Knowledge will give you power, but character respect."
— Bruce Lee

SUMMARY
Please write your demonstration of self-love today.

"They cannot take away our self-respect if we do not give it to them."

– Mahatma Gandhi

Self-respect | ˌself-ri-ˈspekt | - the pride and confidence in oneself; a feeling that one is behaving with honor and dignity.

- **S** – Solitude is necessary for self-care and self-respect.
- **E** – Embrace who you are and do not allow others to disrespect you.
- **L** – Love who you are and who you're becoming.
- **F** – Flourish and stay focused on your growth.
- **R** – Remember that you choose who you allow in your life, and you are
- **E** – Entitled to give as little access as you'd like to others.
- **S** – Speak positive things into your life, acknowledge the
- **P** – Peaceful and still moments as an opportunity to grow and be the
- **E** – Epitome of your mirror reflection, and be
- **C** – Committed to loving on yourself and giving yourself the best of everything as you
- **T** – Thrive for greatness!

LESSON QUESTIONS

What have you done to practice self-respect?

_____

_____

Provide here a demonstration of self-respect.

_____

_____

365 ON ME QUESTIONNAIRE

1. Have you allowed others to disrespect you because you didn't respect yourself?
   Yes
   No
   Undecided

REMINDER

You teach people how to treat you. You also teach yourself how to treat yourself so be kind and gentle with yourself.

— Bianca G.

"When someone treats you like an option, help them narrow their choices by removing yourself from the equation. It's that simple."

— Unknown

INSPIRATIONAL QUOTE

"Respect yourself enough to walk away from anything that no longer serves you, grows you, or makes you happy."

— Robert Tew

SUMMARY

Please write your demonstration of self-love today.

_____

_____

_____

_____

_____

_____

_____

_____

_____

Allow yourself to feel. One that feels can believe, and when you believe, you will have the ability to change what needs to be changed.

— Bianca G.

Feel | ˈfelt | - to be aware of (a person or object) through touching or being touched.

Complete the following sentences by selecting a feeling word if it applies, and if not, use one from your thoughts:

Frustrated	Angry	Happy	Sad	Lonely	Cheerful
Jealous	Exhausted	Curious	Annoyed	Silly	Disappointed
Hopeful	Disgusted	Proud	Shocked		

I feel _____ when I'm with someone I care about.
I feel _____ because I am starting a new chapter in my life.
I feel _____ sometimes, and I don't know why.
I feel _____ when I can share my thoughts and true feelings with others.
I feel _____ when I don't have anyone to talk to about my problems.

LESSON QUESTION
What feeling word would you use to describe your current feelings? (ie happy, angry, excited, lonely, cheerful, etc)

_____

_____

What feelings would you like to feel instead of another?

_____

_____

REMINDER
"Sometimes, your best feelings are found in the words which you type and never send."
— Unknown

INSPIRATIONAL QUOTE

"Feelings help us to identify some things about ourselves that we didn't know we'd possess without experiencing certain situations."
— Unknown

SUMMARY

Please write your demonstration of self-love today.

_____
_____
_____
_____
_____
_____
_____
_____
_____
_____
_____
_____
_____
_____

"The quality of a person's life is in direct proportion to their commitment to excellence, regardless of their chosen field of endeavor."

— Vince Lombardi

Commitment | kə-ˈmit-mənt | - the state or quality of being dedicated to a cause, activity, etc.

LESSON QUESTIONS
What areas of your life have you committed to growth?

_____

_____

Name three reasons you are committed to improving these areas of your life.

1. _____

2. _____

3. _____

365 ON ME QUESTIONNAIRE

1. Are you committed to making pertinent changes in your life?
    Yes
    No
    Undecided

2. Does commitment scare you because it is something that requires loyalty to yourself?
    Yes
    No
    Undecided

REMINDER
To be committed to something is to give it your all, and no matter what happens, you do not change your mind.

— Bianca G.

INSPIRATIONAL QUOTE
"Commitment unlocks the doors of imagination, allows vision, and gives us the right stuff to turn our dream into reality."

– James Womack

SUMMARY
Please write your demonstration of self-love today.

"You have the ability to choose your actions. You have been gifted with life and soul."
— Ramon Luis

"It's not enough to be very good if you have the ability to be great."
— Pam Farrel

Ability | ə-ˈbi-lə-tē | - possession of the means or skill to do something.

In your own words, what is the meaning of ability?

_____

_____

DAILY AFFIRMATIONS
Believe in yourself.
Ability is what you're capable of doing.
Patience is not simply the ability to wait—it's how we behave while we're waiting.
For success, attitude is equally as important as ability.
— Bianca G.

365 ON ME QUESTIONNAIRE
1. Have I explored my full potential to complete a specific task?
   Yes
   No
   Undecided

2. Am I allowing past unfortunate experiences to deter me from attempting to complete new goals?
   Yes
   No
   Undecided

REMINDER
Go out into the world and do things you've never done, never thought about doing, and didn't know you could do. Your ability lies in your effort, my friend.
— Bianca G.

INSPIRATIONAL QUOTE
"It's very easy to be different, but very difficult to be better."
— Jonathan Ive

Write your inspirational quote:
_____
_____

SUMMARY
Please write your demonstration of self-love today.
_____
_____
_____
_____
_____
_____
_____
_____
_____
_____
_____
_____
_____

"Elevation requires separation. Evolution demands change.

— Bianca G.

"Evolution is the most popular way we have of dealing with change."

— Seth Godin

Evolution | ˌe-və-ˈlü-shən | - the process by which different kinds of living organisms are thought to have developed and diversified from earlier forms during the history of the earth. (2) The gradual development of something, especially from a simple to a more complex form.

LESSON QUESTION

What is your strongest asset? (i.e. your ability to adapt, change, evolve, etc.)

___

Name two ways you and/or two areas in your life have evolved.

___

___

What areas in your life demand change?

___

___

REMINDER

"It is not the strongest of the species that survive, nor the most intelligent, but the one most responsive to change."
— Chorus Darwin

INSPIRATIONAL QUOTE

"We are the facilitators of our own creative evolution."
— Bill Hicks

"Time is change, transformation, evolution."
— I.L. Peretz

SUMMARY
Please write your demonstration of self-love today.

"The greater the impact you want to make, the greater your influence needs to be."

– Lolly Daskal

Impact | ˈim-ˌpakt | - the action of one object coming forcibly into contact with another. (2) Have a strong effect on someone or something.

I – Influence gives the capacity to have an effect in the most
M – modest and mindful way
P – possible to not only show that you're influential, but
A – authentic, ambitious, and amazingly
C – committed to enhancing the lives of others while
T – thriving to be your best self for yourself.

Recreate your IMPACT

I – _____
M – _____
P – _____
A – _____
C – _____
T – _____

LESSON QUESTIONS

What are two influential impacts you have had on others?

_____

_____

In what ways have you had an impact on your own life?

_____

_____

REMINDER

"Every action we take impacts the lives of others around us. The question is: Are you aware of your impact?"

– Arthur Carmazzi

INSPIRATIONAL QUOTE
"Everything you do has some effect, some impact."
— Dalai Lama

SUMMARY
Please write your demonstration of self-love today.

_____
_____
_____
_____
_____
_____
_____
_____
_____
_____
_____
_____
_____
_____
_____

"Nurture your relationships just like you nurture a plant. And not just your relationships with others, but your relationship with yourself, too."

– Healing Mind

Nurture | ˈnər-chər | - the care and attention given to someone or something that is growing or developing.

DAILY AFFIRMATIONS
I value my relationships.
Good relationships are good for my health.
My relationships help me get through stressful situations.
I can influence the world positively with my relationships.

– Bianca G.

Write four of your daily affirmations on nurturing relationships:

1. _____

2. _____

3. _____

4. _____

LESSON QUESTIONS
What does it mean to nurture your relationships with others?

_____

_____

Describe one way you have nurtured your relationship with yourself.

_____

_____

365 ON ME QUESTIONNAIRE

1. Have I truly given my all to nurture my partner or friend in our relationship?
   Yes
   No
   Undecided

REMINDER

While caring and loving others, don't forget to water your flowers. You are the most important person to yourself.

— Bianca G.

INSPIRATIONAL QUOTE

"Be the one who nurtures and builds. Be the one who has an understanding and a forgiving heart, one who looks for the best in people. Leave people better than you found them."

— Marvin J. Ashton

SUMMARY

Please write your demonstration of self-love today.

_____
_____
_____
_____
_____
_____
_____
_____

"Proper preparation prevents poor performance."

– Unknown

Preparation | ˌpre-pə-ˈrā-shən | - the action or process of making ready or being made ready for use or consideration.

DAILY AFFIRMATIONS

The best preparation for tomorrow is doing your best today.
There are no secrets to success.
The best preparation for good work tomorrow is to do good work today.
A strong, positive self-image is the best possible preparation for success.
— Bianca G.

Write four of your daily affirmations on preparation:

1. _____

2. _____

3. _____

4. _____

Complete by inputting your words
Today is an opportunity to _____ and to prepare for tomorrow. When tomorrow comes, I will _____ and _____ to _____. Because I've prepared myself, _____. This also creates commitment and _____ in other areas of my life.

signed _____

LESSON QUESTIONS

What is the single most important thing you've prepared for?

_____

List three different areas of your life that require preparation.

_____

_____

_____

REMINDER
"Before anything else, preparation is the key to success."
— Alexander Graham Bell

INSPIRATIONAL QUOTE
"If you are going to achieve excellence in big things, you develop the habit in little matters. Excellence is not an exception, it is a prevailing attitude."
— Colin Powell

SUMMARY
Please write your demonstration of self-love today.

_____

_____

_____

_____

_____

_____

_____

_____

"Like the butterfly, I have the strength and hope to believe (that) in time, I will emerge from my cocoon... transformed."

— The Social Butterfly

Transformation sometimes requires separation. During this time of your life, you may experience many challenges that will determine your ability to accept change. Change may mean that some people cannot go where you're headed.

— Bianca G.

Transformation | ˌtran(t)s-fər-ˈmā-shən | - a thorough or dramatic change in form or appearance.

Complete by inputting your words

In order to fly, _____ and _____ must happen. I have to allow myself to _____ so that when change happens, I am _____. Learning to spread my wings, will be _____ for me and now its time to fly.

signed _____

Create two inspirational quotes on transformation:

_____

_____

365 ON ME QUESTIONNAIRE

1. Have you fully embraced your ability to change even when things are difficult?
   Yes
   No
   Undecided

2. Are there areas in your life that demand transformation, but you haven't allowed the necessary changes?
   Yes
   No
   Undecided

Write three challenges that you face(d) when attempting transformation. After writing out challenges, place an 'X' on the challenges that no longer exist and replace them with the futures you transformed. (Example: Challenge - accepting constructive criticism, Future Me - being open-minded and teachable)

Challenge	Future Me
_____	_____
_____	_____
_____	_____

REMINDER
"Nothing happens until the pain of remaining the same outweighs the pain of change."
– Arthur Burt

INSPIRATIONAL QUOTE
"Transformation isn't about adding more work to your life; it is about shifting your perspective so life becomes more fun, magical, and joyful."
– Sheri Salata

SUMMARY
Please write your demonstration of self-love today.

_____

_____

_____

_____

_____

"Every sunset is an opportunity to reset."

– Unknown

Reset | (ˌ)rē-ˈset | - to set again or differently.

Rewrite your REs

"RE - Set"   RE - _____

"RE - Align"   RE - _____

"RE - Start"   RE - _____

"RE - Claim"   RE - _____

"RE - Ignite"   RE - _____

For every "RE", add an inspirational word (i.e., Relive - Freedom, Readjust - change)

Refresh – _____

Renew – _____

Recharge – _____

Refocus – _____

LESSON QUESTION

What areas of your life demand a reset?

_____

_____

_____

_____

365 ON ME QUESTIONNAIRE

1. Have you ignored signs of a much-needed reset or change in your life?
   Yes
   No
   Undecided

REMINDER
Write your reminder:

_____

_____

— Signed _____

"Never restart a journey and use the same road that failed you before."
— Unknown

INSPIRATIONAL QUOTE
"Everyone must choose one of two pains: the pain of discipline or the pain of regret."
— Unknown

SUMMARY
Please write your demonstration of self-love today.

To improve is to change; to become is to change; to develop is to change; therefore, transitioning will require a new you.

– Bianca G.

Transition | tran(t)-ˈsi-shən | - the process or a period of changing from one state or condition to another.

Name five words that come to mind when you think of transition/transitioning:

_____   _____   _____

_____   _____

LESSON QUESTIONS

Have you started your life's transition and stopped for a specific reason? If so, what is/was this reason?

_____

_____

If you haven't started your transition, when will you start?

_____

What is the purpose of transitioning?

_____

_____

365 ON ME QUESTIONNAIRE

1. Have you not transitioned because of fear?
    Yes
    No
    Undecided

2. Does transitioning require you to end and/or begin a relationship?
    Yes
    No
    Undecided

REMINDER
Write your reminder here:

_____

_____

—Signed _____

"Change is inevitable, growth is optional."

— John. C. Maxwell

INSPIRATIONAL QUOTE
"Any transition serious enough to alter your definition of self will require not just small adjustments in your way of living and thinking but a full-on metamorphosis."

— Martha N. Beck

SUMMARY
Please write your demonstration of self-love today.

_____

_____

_____

_____

_____

_____

_____

_____

"Transparency increases credibility and accountability."

— Park Won-soon

Transparency | tran(t)s-ˈper-ən(t)-sē | - the condition of being transparent. The quality of being done in an open way without secrets.

Define transparency in your own words.
_____

_____

TRANSPARENCY AFFIRMATIONS
I create my happiness.
My challenges are actually opportunities.
My life is filled with an abundance of goodness.
I am beautiful just the way I am.

— Unknown

Write four of your transparency affirmations:
1. _____

2. _____

3. _____

4. _____

365 ON ME QUESTIONNAIRE
1. Are you as transparent with yourself as you should be?
    Yes
    No
    Undecided

2. Have you acknowledged that certain areas of your life require transparency and you haven't addressed them?
    Yes
    No
    Undecided

REMINDER
"Honesty and transparency make you vulnerable. Be honest and transparent anyway."
— Mother Teresa

"Be real. Be honest. Be true and be you."
— Bianca G.

INSPIRATIONAL QUOTE
"A lack of transparency results in distrust and a deep sense of insecurity."
— Dalai Lama

SUMMARY
Please write your demonstration of self-love today.

_____

_____

_____

_____

_____

_____

_____

_____

_____

_____

What is a thought or idea without manifestation? What is a dream without a plan? What is a trip without a destination? What is action without execution?

— Bianca G.

Execution | ˌek-si-ˈkyü-shən | - the carrying out or putting into effect of a plan, order, or course of action.

Today, I, _____ pledge _____

_____

— Signed _____

LESSON QUESTIONS

What are some things that require an execution plan in your life?

_____

_____

What is the fire inside of you that encourages you to fully commit to completing a task with full potential?

_____

_____

REMINDER

"A good plan violently executed now is better than a perfect tomorrow."
— George Patton

INSPIRATIONAL QUOTE

Having a vision is good. Creating a strategy is great. But doing all of the work is wonderful.
— Bianca G.

SUMMARY
Please write your demonstration of self-love today.

"Make your vision so clear that your fears become irrelevant."

— Kerwin Rae

Vision | ˈvi-zhən | - the ability to think about or plan the future with imagination or wisdom.

VISION AFFIRMATIONS
I can see it; therefore, it is mine.
If I can believe it, I can achieve it.
I am a visionary.
I am even more than I see when I look into the mirror.

— Bianca G.

Write four of your vision affirmations:

1. _____

2. _____

3. _____

4. _____

365 ON ME QUESTIONNAIRE

1. Have you allowed your vision to become blurry?
    Yes
    No
    Undecided

2. Will your life require a revision to refocus your vision?
    Yes
    No
    Undecided

Fill in the remainder using your own inspirational words.
   A vision is_____ and_____. As for me, determination,_____ ,_____ , and_____ will take me places that_____ .

– Signed

REMINDER
"It's not what you look at that matters, it's what you see."
– Henry David Thoreau

INSPIRATIONAL QUOTE
"The sky isn't the limit, your vision is."
– Unknown

SUMMARY
Please write your demonstration of self-love today.

_____

_____

_____

_____

_____

_____

_____

_____

Doing something requires action, doing nothing takes up space. Decide if you're going to be active or just breathe.

– Bianca G.

Productivity | ˌprō-dək-ˈti-və-tē | - the effectiveness of productive effort, especially in industry, as measured in terms of the rate of output per unit of input.

One day, during a game I made up called Would You Rather, I asked my 12-year-old client, "Would you rather be a mannequin or a tree?" My conclusion: A tree has roots, a past, a possible future, and with water and sun, it grows. Meanwhile, a mannequin is simply a display that has no ability to move, to speak, to live, but it can just be. Decide if you are a tree or mannequin.

Your decision (tree or mannequin): _____

LESSON QUESTIONS

In what areas are you most productive?

_____

_____

In what areas are you least productive?

_____

_____

List four self-care techniques you'd like to practice.

1. _____
2. _____
3. _____
4. _____

REMINDER
"Focus on being productive instead of busy."
— Tim Ferriss

INSPIRATIONAL QUOTE
"Productivity isn't about being a workhorse. Keeping busy or burning the midnight oil... It's more about priorities, planning, and fiercely protecting your time."
— Gary Keller

SUMMARY
Please write your demonstration of self-love today.

_____

_____

_____

_____

_____

_____

_____

_____

_____

_____

_____

_____

"I am not what happened to me, I am what I choose to become."

– Emma Watson

Pursuit | pur·suit pər-ˈsüt | - the action of following or pursuing someone or something.

    P – Peaceful, poised, and the prodigy of your
    U – understanding of what you can achieve. You're
    R – resilient and radiant, with a
    S – strong hold that demonstrates sagacity with
    U - unlimited uniqueness that projects an
    I - intensifying, impeccable,
    T – take-charge attitude to reach greater heights,

Create your pursuit.
P – _____
U – _____
R – _____
S – _____
U – _____
I – _____
T – _____

LESSON QUESTION

What are you currently in pursuit of in life?
_____
_____

What have you attempted to pursue, and things didn't quite go as planned?
_____
_____
_____
_____
_____

365 ON ME QUESTIONNAIRE

1. Is there one single thing that you feel is holding you back from completing something important?

    Yes
    No
    Undecided

REMINDER

"Don't ever let somebody tell you, you can't do something, not even me. You got a dream, you gotta protect it. People can't do something themselves, they want to tell you that you can't do it."

— Chris Garner (Will Smith)

INSPIRATIONAL QUOTE

"Still a dreamer, yet more of a realist than ever before, I knew this was my time to sail. On the horizon, I saw the shining future, as before. The difference now was that I felt the wind at my back. I was ready."

— Unknown

SUMMARY

Please write your demonstration of self-love today.

_____
_____
_____
_____
_____
_____
_____
_____

"Stability is everything, be it emotional or physical. You need a solid ground to build anything on."
— Unknown

Stability | stə-ˈbi-lə-tē | - the state of being stable.

What does it mean for you to be stable in the ways listed below?

Mentally stable _____

Emotionally stable _____

Physically stable _____

Spiritually stable _____

Financially stable _____

LESSON QUESTION
List your areas of stability from strongest to least strong.

_____

_____

365 ON ME QUESTIONNAIRE

1. Have you recovered from a perturbational experience in your life?
   Yes
   No
   Undecided

2. Have you encountered trials that interrupt(ed) your ability to remain mentally or emotionally stable?
   Yes
   No
   Undecided

List four self-care techniques you'd like to practice.

1. _____

2. _____

3. _____

4. _____

REMINDER
"In order to find stability in the world, we must first find it in ourselves."
— Tyler J. Hebert

When something or someone isn't adding to your life, learn how to subtract what doesn't create consistency, loyalty, change, and stability in your life.
— Bianca G.

INSPIRATIONAL QUOTE
"You are only as mentally tough as your life demands you to be. An easy life fashions a mind that can only handle ease. A challenging life builds a mind that can handle a challenge. Like a muscle that atrophies without use, mental strength fades unless it is tested. When life doesn't challenge you, challenge yourself."
— James Clear

SUMMARY
Please write your demonstration of self-love today.

_____

_____

_____

_____

_____

"Science is simply the word we use to describe a method of organizing our curiosity."
— Tim Minchin

Intrigue | ˈin-ˌtrēg | - the curiosity or interest of; fascinate.

INTRIGUE AFFIRMATIONS

I am free.
I am free to choose how I experience my experiences.
I am from anything that is positive.
I am present in my freedom.
—Bianca G.

Create four of your own intrigue affirmations.

1. _____

2. _____

3. _____

4. _____

LESSON QUESTIONS

What are the three most intriguing things/interests you have?

_____

_____

_____

What intrigues and/or piques your interest in this life?

_____

_____

REMINDER

"Nothing has such power to broaden the mind as the ability to investigate systematically and truly all that comes under thy observation in life."
— Marcus Aurelius

INSPIRATIONAL QUOTE

"Wisdom requires not only the investigation of many things, but contemplation of the mystery."

— Jeremy Narby

SUMMARY

Please write your demonstration of self-love today.

"You have to envision yourself winning to win."

— Keith Ferrazzi

Envision | in-ˈvi-zhən | - the image as a future possibility; visualize.

ENVISION AFFIRMATIONS

"Create the highest, grandest vision possible for your life, because you become what you believe."

— Oprah Winfrey

"We don't create our future life in the future. We don't create it tomorrow, or later this week, or next month. We create it now. We create it today."

— Envision

Write your envision affirmation:

_____

_____

— Signed _____

LESSON QUESTION

What have you envisioned for your future self?

_____

_____

Name two things you see in your future.
1. _____

2. _____

365 ON ME QUESTIONNAIRE

1. Have you upheld your future plans for others?
   - Yes
   - No
   - Undecided

2. When you envision your future self, does that include your current plans to succeed?
   Yes
   No
   Undecided

REMINDERS

"If you talk about it, it's a dream. If you envision it, it's possible. But if you schedule it, it's real."
— Tony Robbins

"When you envision yourself doing something, you'll be surprised at how much that helps you to actually do it."
— Selim Nurudeen

INSPIRATIONAL QUOTE

Imagine yourself being your best self, and showing up as that every time.
— Bianca G.

SUMMARY

Please write your demonstration of self-love today.

_____

_____

_____

_____

_____

_____

_____

Handle yourself diligently. Take care of your mental, emotional, and spiritual health. You deserve to be healthy.

— Bianca G.

Diligence | ˈdi-lə-jən(t)s | - careful and persistent work or effort.

Below are words that come to mind when thinking of diligence. Write the meaning of each word, and create a quote using your words and diligence.

Quality – _____
_____
_____

Effort – _____
_____
_____

Strive – _____
_____
_____

Goal – _____
_____
_____

Commit – _____
_____
_____

Purpose – _____
_____
_____

Your Quote _____
_____
_____

— Signed _____

LESSON QUESTION
What does due diligence mean to you?

_____

_____

What are some ways you have worked diligently?

_____

_____

365 ON ME QUESTIONNAIRE
1. Have you worked diligently on creating a better future for yourself?
   Yes
   No
   Undecided

REMINDER
"Focus means being diligent. Diligence always leads to wealth."
—Sunday Adelaja

INSPIRATIONAL QUOTE
"There is no barrier to success that diligence and perseverance cannot hurdle."
– Oscar Micheaux

SUMMARY
Please write your demonstration of self-love today.

_____

_____

_____

_____

"The most effective teachers embody the teaching they give out."

– Maharishi Mahiesh Yogi.

Embody |selfxxx| - to be an expression of or give a tangible or visible form to (an idea, quality, or feeling).

Please complete the following statements: (Example: Embody demonstrates wholeness.)

Embody feels like _____

Embody means to _____

Embody allows _____

Embody represent _____

LESSON QUESTION
In what ways have you embodied your whole self?

_____

_____

365 ON ME QUESTIONNAIRE
1. Have you acknowledged your ability to embrace and embody your success and/or accomplishments?
    Yes
    No
    Undecided

REMINDER
"Don't explain your philosophy. Embody it."
– Epictetus

INSPIRATIONAL QUOTE
"It's not what happens to you, but how you react to it that matters."
– Epictetus

SUMMARY
Please write your demonstration of self-love today.

"Sometimes, things aren't clear right away. That's where you need to be patient and preserve and see where things lead."

— Mary Pierce

Patience | ˈpā-shən(t)s | - the capacity to accept or tolerate delay, trouble, or suffering without getting angry or upset.

DAILY AFFIRMATIONS

I breathe in stillness and peace and breathe out anxiety.
Patience is a skill I can learn through practice.
I can control my thoughts more and more every day.
I am more patient than I have ever been before.

Create four daily patience affirmations for yourself:
1. _____
2. _____
3. _____
4. _____

— Signed _____

LESSON QUESTION

What are you currently working on that requires patience?
_____
_____

In what areas of your life have you lacked patience?
_____
_____

365 ON ME QUESTIONNAIRE

1. Has having patience helped you to get specific tasks done?
    Yes
    No
    Undecided

2. Are there specific areas in your life that require more time, investment, and patience than others?
    Yes
    No
    Undecided

REMINDER
"The secret of patience is to do something else in the meantime."
— Croft M. Pentz

INSPIRATIONAL QUOTE
"Patience is the calm acceptance that things can happen in a different order than the one you have in your mind."
— Unknown

SUMMARY
Please write your demonstration of self-love today.

_____
_____
_____
_____
_____
_____

"The practice of assertiveness: being authentic in our dealings with others; treating our values and persons with decent respect in social contexts; refusing to fake the reality of who we are or what we esteem in order to avoid disapproval; the willingness to stand up for ourselves and our ideas in appropriate ways in appropriate contexts."

– Nathaniel Branden

Assertive |ə-ˈsər-tiv| - having or showing a confident and forceful personality.

I. You have the right to judge your behavior, thoughts, and emotions, and to take the responsibility for their initiation and consequences upon yourself.
II. You have the right to offer no reasons or excuses for justifying your behavior.
III. You have the right to judge if you are responsible for finding solutions to other people's problems.
IV. You have the right to change your mind.
V. You have the right to make mistakes—and be responsible for them.
VI. You have the right to say, "I don't know."
VII. You have the right to be independent of the goodwill of others before coping with them.
VIII. You have the right to be illogical in making decisions.
IX. You have the right to say, "I don't understaxnd."
X. You have the right to say, "I don't care."

You have the right to say no without feeling guilty.

LESSON QUESTION

In what ways are you assertive? If you haven't recognized any, in what ways would you like to be assertive?

_____

_____

_____

What do you think is required for you to adopt assertive characteristics?

_____

_____

REMINDER
Be real, be free, and be you.

— Bianca G.

INSPIRATIONAL QUOTE
Speak your words boldly, confidently, and respectfully. How others receive things isn't your responsibility. However your delivery is pertinent.

— Bianca G.

SUMMARY
Please write your demonstration of self-love today.

_____

_____

_____

_____

_____

_____

_____

_____

_____

_____

_____

_____

"The pursuit, even of the best things, ought to be calm and tranquil."

– Marcus Tullius Cicero

Tranquility | tran-ˈkwi-lə-tē | - the quality or state of being tranquil; calm.

T – Therapeutic experiences offer
R – relaxation, readiness, and relentless
A – ability to adapt, achieve, and appreciate assurgent and
N – necessary calmness to acknowledge
Q – quietness and pureness with an
U – unparalleled, unwavering freedom when the world doesn't seem to care; yet, we are allowed to experience this
I – impeccable moment to
L – laugh, live, and love however and whenever we choose.

365 ON ME QUESTIONNAIRE

1. Have you allowed yourself to enjoy or fully emerge in tranquility?
   Yes
   No
   Undecided

2. Are you open to improving your tranquil and/or calm experience?
   Yes
   No
   Undecided

REMINDER

"When we are unable to find tranquility within ourselves, it is useless to seek it elsewhere."

– Francois de La Rachefoucauld

INSPIRATIONAL QUOTE

"Tranquility is a choice. So is anxiety. The entire world around us may be in turmoil, but if we want to be peaceful within, we can."

– Unknown

SUMMARY
Please write your demonstration of self-love today.

To understand the importance of ability, one must possess enough courage to believe in possibility, too.
— Bianca G.

Possibility | ˌpä-sə-ˈbi-lə-tē | - a thing that may happen or be the case.

Positive words are associated with possibility. Fill in the blanks to add more.

Potentially	Hope	_____	_____
_____		Capability	Contingence	Possibility
Eventuality	Surety	_____	_____
_____		Opportunity	Prospect	Certainty

LESSON QUESTION
Name two ways you have turned doubt into possibility.

1. _____

2. _____

List three examples of your possibility turned into reality.

1. _____

2. _____

3. _____

365 ON ME QUESTIONNAIRE
1. Have you allowed doubt to outweigh possibility due to past failures?
   Yes
   No
   Undecided

REMINDER
"In order to obtain the impossible, one must attempt the absurd."
— Miquel de Cervantes

INSPIRATIONAL QUOTE
"Do not become so attached to any one belief that you cannot see past it to another possibility."

– Christopher Padlini

SUMMARY
Please write your demonstration of self-love today.

_____

_____

_____

_____

_____

_____

_____

_____

_____

_____

_____

_____

_____

"Be brave, take risks, and allow the unexpected."

— Unknown

Bravery | ˈbrāv-rē | - courageous behavior or character.

I am hopeful in all things.
My ability to take risks is my strength.
I will allow unexpected things to happen.
I am allowed to be free.

Write four additional bravery affirmations:

1. _____

2. _____

3. _____

4. _____

LESSON QUESTION

List the ways you have taken a risk on each of the below.

Education – _____

love life – _____

Finances – _____

Work-life – _____

In what ways do you want to become braver?
_____
_____

365 ON ME QUESTIONNAIRE

1. Have you allowed your personal issues to hinder you from making important decisions?
    Yes
    No
    Undecided

REMINDER
"I learned that courage was not the absence of fear, but the triumph over it. The brave man is not he who does not feel afraid, but he who conquers that fear."
— Nelson Mandela

INSPIRATIONAL QUOTE
"Bravery is the audacity to be unhindered by failures and to walk with freedom, strength, and hope in the face of things unknown."
— Unknown

SUMMARY
Please write your demonstration of self-love today.

_____
_____
_____
_____
_____
_____
_____
_____
_____
_____
_____
_____

"I am receptive to the inflow and outpouring of the universe."

– Eric Butterworth

Receptive | ri-ˈsep-tiv | - willing to consider or accept new suggestions and ideas.

Identify other positive words that are associated with the word *receptive*.

Willingness Open-mindedness New ideas Suggestive

LESSON QUESTION

In what ways have you been receptive in different said areas of your life?

Intimate relationships – _____

Family life – _____

Educational goals – _____

Friendships – _____

365 ON ME QUESTIONNAIRE

1. Are you aware of your potential to change and/or open your mind to trying new things?
    Yes
    No
    Undecided

REMINDER

Open your mind and allow change to help you grow and develop.

Write your reminder:

_____
_____

— Signed _____

INSPIRATIONAL QUOTE
"It is as impossible to withhold education from the receptive mind, as it is impossible to force it upon the unreasoning."
— Agnes Repplier

Write your inspirational quote:

_____
_____

— Signed _____

SUMMARY
Please write your demonstration of self-love today.

_____
_____
_____
_____
_____
_____

"Be modest. It's an admirable quality that not many people possess."

– Polka Doti

Modest | ˈmä-dəst | - unassuming or moderate in the estimation of one's abilities or achievements.

M – Mindfully and meritoriously become
O – omnipotent in your ways to
D – develop a dauntless strength that surpasses anything that tries to hinder my
E – eagerness and enthusiastic abilities to grow and
S – shine, even during
T – tough times, because I know that triumph will come.

Write your M.O.D.E.S.T.
M – _____
O – _____
D – _____
E – _____
S – _____
T – _____

LESSON QUESTION

Identify three ways you have experienced modesty.
1. _____

2. _____

3. _____

Identify three ways you need to develop modesty.
1. _____

2. _____

3. _____

REMINDER
"Modesty isn't about covering up our own bodies because they're bad; modesty isn't about hiding ourselves; it's about revealing our dignity."
— Jessica Rey

INSPIRATIONAL QUOTE
"True modesty does not consist in an ignorance of our merits, but in a due estimate of them."
— A. W. Hare

SUMMARY
Please write your demonstration of self-love today.

_____
_____
_____
_____
_____
_____
_____
_____
_____
_____

Set yourself free! Allow yourself to feel, to believe, to experience, to fail, to live and to just be.

– Bianca G.

Freedom | ˈfrē-dəm | - the power or right to act, speak, or think as one wants without hindrance or restraint.

In your own words, what is the meaning of freedom?
_____
_____

Complete the statement below:
To emerge unconsciously in my _____ will allow me peace and _____ . To emerge consciously in my _____ will allow me peace and _____ .

LESSON QUESTION
In what ways are you free?
_____
_____

In what ways do you want to be free?
_____
_____

365 ON ME QUESTIONNAIRE

1. Have you allowed yourself to experience true freedom in your life?
    Yes
    No
    Undecided

2. Are you afraid or hesitant about being free in certain areas of your life?
    Yes
    No
    Undecided

REMINDER
"Freedom is not worth having if it does not include the freedom to make mistakes."
— Mahatma Gandhi

INSPIRATIONAL QUOTE
"I know but one freedom, and that is the freedom of the mind."
— Antoine de Saint-Exupéry

SUMMARY
Please write your demonstration of self-love today.

_____

_____

_____

_____

_____

_____

_____

_____

_____

_____

_____

_____

365 ON ME QUESTIONNAIRE EXPANSION

365 ON ME QUESTIONNAIRE EXPANSION

365 ON ME QUESTIONNAIRE EXPANSION

365 ON ME QUESTIONNAIRE EXPANSION

365 ON ME QUESTIONNAIRE EXPANSION

365 ON ME QUESTIONNAIRE EXPANSION

Note From The Author

With great gratitude, I wanted to extend my appreciation for you purchasing and reading my very first workbook. It is my hope that you have learned some new things about yourself, acknowledged areas of growth, and become more aware of the importance of continuous education on self. Whether this book was gifted by someone to you or if you personally chose it, I believe that if skills and education are applied, you will start to identify strengths that you already possess, however, this book is a reminder of how amazing you are with new tools and skills.

"Wherever you go in this life, may you discover beautiful things, places, and people that are just as eager as you are to share one world with many different colors, peace, hope, understanding, and love."

– Bianca G.

www.ingramcontent.com/pod-product-compliance
Lightning Source LLC
Chambersburg PA
CBHW061110070526
44583CB00027B/3249